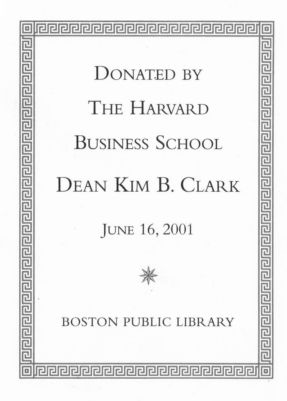

a · plain · life

By Scott Savage

The Plain Reader (editor)

A Plain Life

a · plain · life
walking my belief

Scott Savage

Ballantine Books · New York

A Ballantine Book
The Ballantine Publishing Group

Copyright © 2000 by Scott Savage

A record of the Library of Congress Catalog Card Number is
available upon request from the publisher.

Text design by Holly Johnson
Illustration copyright © 2000 by Chuck Trapkus

Manufactured in the United States of America

10   9   8   7   6   5   4   3

To Mary Ann

STRENGTH AND HONOR
ARE HER CLOTHING

—Proverbs 31:25

"BE ONE!"

An agent of the Bureau of Motor Vehicles shouts out my ticket number—B-1. I hurry through rows of folding chairs to the front of the room, underneath the scrutiny of security cameras trained on the waiting area. There a man in white slacks and tunic points me to the right, on past the place where they are taking digital photographs for licenses. I find an empty seat along a partitioned counter. My final destination.

A young woman, "Maria" according to her name tag, is across from me, her placid features partly hidden behind a computer monitor. Without looking up, she asks how she can help me.

"I want to have my driver's license revoked," I reply as casually as I can, hoping to make it sound like a reasonable request.

A wide, amused smile dips out from behind the computer. Slipping free from the routine of generating new licenses, renewing old ones, and issuing temporary permits, she actually looks at her current customer.

"You want it . . . revoked?" Maria's voice trails off and

her eyes widen slightly as she really takes me in: my broad-brimmed straw hat, collarless shirt, leather suspenders, and long beard.

Am I Amish? Am I a time traveler from the 1850s? Whichever, something strange is going on here. But this is the biggest motor vehicle office in the state, and a lot of unusual people must come through here; I see that Maria is regaining her composure and her smile already. Only now her head is tilted forward and her tranquil eyebrows are poised in a question.

"Yes," I tell her once more, "I really want to give it back." Now I'm smiling back at her.

It's in my hand, the piece of plastic that brought me here on an eight-day walking journey. Setting the license on the counter turns up to the harsh office lights the small color photo in the upper right corner. A clean-shaven, modern face, self-confidently looking the world in the eye. But it isn't my face anymore. So yes, here it is, please take it back.

This is my Big Moment, the supposed culmination of my 120-mile pilgrimage on foot from my tiny Quaker community to this large city. But I always knew I wouldn't get to make a speech or anything when the time came. Just hand the license to Maria now and smile.

I'd like to tell her that while I am not Amish, I do live in much the same way they do. In a few days I'll be back home mucking out the horse's stall, planting my potatoes and peas, hauling wood for next winter. If the weather is nice, one evening I'll be walking barefoot to midweek Quaker meeting with my wife and children.

I could explain that I used to wear a suit and sit in

front of a computer screen, that I made an hour-long commute to work. That nowadays I get around slowly by horse and buggy, and I like it a lot better.

As for the license and why I walked such a distance to give it away, the walk itself has given me the answer, and what the walk told me is this: Our souls require boundaries beyond which we are not known to any but our Maker. Being known at a remove—as, for example, information in the data banks of society—makes us less than we really are.

Even more important, the walk confirmed my belief that our modern individualist sense of freedom conspires with our easy, car-based mobility to blind us to our need for one another, for community, for God.

Maria, I might sum up, I'm here to prepare for my return to a sense of place.

But actually we just smile at one another. That says almost as much, anyway.

Taking my license in her hand, Maria wonders aloud if I really *can* return it. Before I can think to reply, she turns to an older woman at the next partition who is busily stacking computer-printed registration forms:

"Hey, Marti, can he *do* that?"

Apparently Marti has overheard our conversation, because she instantly looks over her shoulder and barks out to the man in white: "LAZLO! 'REQUEST FOR CANCELLATION OF DRIVING PRIVILEGES'! BACK OF THE BOTTOM DRAWER IN THE SHORT CABINET!"

People say that when it comes to the government, there's a form for everything. I guess it's true.

"Here ya go, Sis." Lazlo hands Maria a half sheet of paper. Maria begins to explain to me how to fill it out, but as she looks more closely at my license her smile disappears again in confusion.

"But your license expires today!"

Well, I know that. Practically speaking, I never had to come here. If I don't want to have a license, all I have to do is let it expire, which is what it is doing even as we speak. I tell her that I still need to cancel it, and we sit staring at each other for another few seconds before she smiles again. She has figured out this is something I have to do for reasons other than the practical, and that seems to please her. Even if I am—maybe—a nut.

Dating and signing the form, I hand it back and wait for my copy. I feel something rising up in me like a song. Belief, I'm thinking, even when it's sometimes silent or even invisible, can accomplish God's will in the most amazing fashion. That's a bit of wisdom I can take back with me in place of my driver's license, when I leave this room and this city to return to a plain life. . . .

a · plain · life

Places on the Map

Meeting for worship always ends slowly. In its last stage, bodies seated on the rough and simple benches may begin to shift from their formerly still postures, or the sound of a shoe unconsciously dragged against the dark wooden floor will interrupt the final stretch of silence, and at one of these physical signs of stirring, eyes that had been gazing down at those same well-oiled planks for a long time will lift up, look around, and eventually rest on the bonneted face of the clerk of the meeting. And when it seems right, she will turn to the person seated next to her—on the day in question it happened to be my wife—clasp her hand, and bring the time of worship to a close.

On that day a very few of the Friends present (or Quakers, as they're often called) had stood at one time or another with some words of ministry. One of those who spoke had been the fellow seated in front of me, a young man in a wide-brimmed black felt hat who, I saw, was now standing at the door to the next room, excitedly motioning for me to follow. When I caught up to him on the far side of the partition he was rummaging through some books and papers piled on top of a tall cabinet that was almost the match for his own lanky reach. Carefully he brought down a long, scroll-like sheet of rolled-up paper and took it to a table near the window.

I saw as I helped him unroll it that the scroll was covered with an intricately drawn mass of blue-black lines—tubes, really, with writing all around and in them— a plumbing diagram that began with a single stout pipe at the left-hand edge marked "First Generation of Friends, London Yearly Meeting, 1668," and reached across the page in a tangled anarchy to where my hand partly covered the final date, 1985.

It was a blueprint of the history of the Religious Society of Friends—the Quakers—showing the junctures and divisions over the flow of centuries. A detailed genealogical outline showing separation after separation as affiliations shifted and congregations broke away or redefined their beliefs. Some lines ended where groupings had gone fallow, and other lines began where new ones had formed.

Seth, the young man at my side, was not merely some generic Quaker, but was himself a representative of a particular incarnation to be found somewhere on the diagram before us. He was a "plain" Friend: one who lived and dressed in a way that consciously didn't conform to the larger culture around him. "Plain" Friends were themselves only a subset within the religiously "Conservative" congregation my wife and I were about to join.

Seth's finger rested on the starting point of the earliest Friends and then traced a single "pipe" straight across the middle of the page. The width of the pipe narrowed as other pipes split off above or below it; small, neat handwriting indicated the point in time where each group departed from some essential element of the founding theology. Every new pipe gained a formal title to distinguish it from other sections of the Society, along with a nickname derived from the supposed instigator of the division: Hicksite, Beanite, Maulite, Gurneyite, Otisite . . . too many "-ites" to name.

Following his continuing trajectory along the main line, I saw that it, too, picked up new names: Orthodox, and later Conservative. At the end of the chart only a small vessel carried on in the original direction. A tiny name trickled from its terminus: Wilburite.

Seth smiled wryly and expressed an opinion in his native Carolina drawl.

"Ah think that fellow who drew the map must be a Wilburite, too."

A Wilburite, after John Wilbur, known only for his determination to stick with the faith and practices of the earliest Quakers. Seth was a Wilburite. So would I be, too, soon enough. Glancing over the plumbing diagram, I recognized the names of several other pipes I had started down a few years before, false starts. The Quakerism of previous centuries I read of in books—books written by and about the early Friends who inspired me with their earnest daily practice of Christianity and their mystical approach to worship—*that* Quakerism was to be found today only in a few old meetinghouses in Ohio and Virginia.

My wife, Mary Ann, joined our examination of the scroll, popping our sleeping two-year-old son, Jack, into my arms in order to trace for herself the unbroken line.

Meanwhile, our almost-four-year-old daughter, Natasha, buzzed in wide circles around us, boundless energy and faultless memory in hyperdrive as she recited long bits of Dr. Seuss.

"Oh, now I see. The Wilburites are the One True Religion," Mary Ann said, playfully disapproving. Then, more earnestly, "Seth, don't you think there are different paths people take to find Jesus?"

Seth's eyebrows rose in mock self-defense.

"Ah reckon so. 'In mah father's house there's many mansions.' "

"So there are." A slowly blooming smile came as a reward for having passed Mary Ann's antifanatic test. She had never, ever been moved to join any kind of organization before, and she wanted to be sure about this one. Now her own index finger was tracing softly and unhurriedly backward across the page, finding the way back to the life of "primitive Christianity revived" that was the starting point for the Quakers.

"But still it's nice to have a map of our particular route," she added.

That day spent in a small meetinghouse in Ohio was near the end of the year 1994. Two years earlier we had met Seth, at a time when we were beginning a journey that would take us through the 1990s. Since then we have come a long way. We moved our household of children, books, animals, and furniture up and down the state of Ohio as we groped toward a plainer, simpler, more authentic life. In the years since we found Seth and other Wilburite Friends (there are only a handful), this plain life pretty much became our world: family-size gardens, horse-and-buggy travel, long silences, worshipful community, homemade modest clothing, hard physical work, and a constantly deepening affection for the land where we have finally put down roots.

Those who track trends for the commercial media would probably classify us as "downshifters"—but our personal statistics are so extreme that they belie such a mild term. We have gone from being dual-income-no-kids urban professionals to being Amish-like rural folk with a third of the money, a tenth of the possessions, and a houseful of blessed children.

We also hear ourselves referred to by others as "back-to-the-landers," which is certainly true insofar as we really do value rural life and would never want to return to the city. But although we love and treasure the place in southeastern Ohio we now call home, both for its natural beauty and for our relationship to it as keepers of the garden, the fact is we worship the Creator, not the creation, and our real home—the land we want to get "back" to—isn't even on this earth. "Back to the land" also implies hippies from the 1960s heading out for the country, letting themselves go and "doing their own thing," and we don't qualify for that image, either.

"Letting ourselves go" in our family is a rather different process that involves opening ourselves completely to

God's influence and plan for our lives. *That* kind of letting go has led us in a short number of years to the place we now occupy outside of the mainstream.

I can get a touch of vertigo if I think back to the time just before Mary Ann and I began to relinquish our all-too-human wishes and handed our future over to God. We were like two nervous cliff divers, huddled at the edge of the precipice. We didn't yet have the courage or the faith to make such an awesome leap.

In the time before we began our real journey together, the two of us were so alike in some respects it was almost funny. By day we were both public-service bureaucrats, with long commutes and hurried schedules. In our off hours we were both active in environmental causes, both co-op members, both vegetarians. Two weeks before our wedding we were arrested together for blocking the Earth Day festivities at the zoo in Cleveland with our banner unfurled across the entrance to the RainForest building, a $30 million attraction whose construction money could have bought and saved a sizable portion of the real rain forest. (We weren't very convincing as hardened activists; the park rangers thought we were kind of cute and let us go. They even gave us back the banner.)

Whatever our eccentricities, back then we could be described as basically smart, ecologically concerned 1980s yuppies. What changed us from that into what we are now was our pursuit of a more meaningful life together, and the spiritual gifts that our search uncovered along the way.

Mary Ann and I had always shared a great unhappiness with modern American culture. We couldn't find a comfortable place for ourselves amid the shallowness and cynicism masquerading as coolness and irony many of our twenty-something peers bought into. We also didn't like the sheer physical ugliness of modern life. We both valued *old*: old houses, old forests, old neighborhoods, old people. The more we got close to the old, the better we could compare it to the new. And something about new, in the most pervasive way, didn't feel right.

The two of us were working in public libraries, and we pondered this feeling about modernity's not-right-ness even as we toiled along, surrounded by the written record of human knowledge. So it was natural that our own search for answers would begin there, in libraries, where up and down the aisles of philosophy, literature, art, and history there were dozens of authors engaged in the critiquing of modern life. Nights in our little city duplex apartment were lived in the glare of the electric chandelier over the dining table where we read out loud to one another from the piles of borrowed books stacked around us—books about television, technology, medicine, architecture, advertising, the global economy; books that said everything people believed about the goodness and efficiency of modernity was wrong.

Our readings and discussion continued even after we were in bed, and always our conversation came back to its starting point, with the question of how we could go on living in the society we were reading about.

The critiques weren't enough. Yes, they told us we were not alone in our discomfort, but they rarely offered any hope that we could escape the problems they described. We needed answers, so we returned to the shelves to look for them.

Who could tell us how to cope with modern life in the here and now? Who was actually doing that? Our search quickly led us to books about the Amish. There they were in the religion section of the library, the resisters against modernity. Both Mary Ann and I had come in contact with these gentle people around the peripheries of our separate Ohio childhoods. I grew up in Geauga County, near the fourth-largest concentration of Amish people in the United States, and Mary Ann's hometown of Dover was a few miles from the biggest Amish settlement in the world. We'd seen the Amish in their buggies traveling to town to shop, and each of us had been both admiring and afraid of these plainly dressed strangers and their old-fashioned, austere appearance.

We began to read everything we could find about them. We learned what they ate and what they wore and why they would or would not do certain things that other people took for granted. What might previously have seemed inconsistent about their behavior—for example, why did they sometimes ride in cars if they wouldn't drive or own them?—turned out not to be inconsistent after all. (We learned that the ban on operating cars wasn't an inexplicable taboo, but rather a carefully thought-out defense against the breakdown of community caused by instant and always-available mobility. Taking an occasional taxi ride didn't have the same potential for drastic effect.)

The most important thing we learned, however, was the big "why" of Amish life, which all but a few of books about them seemed to overlook: Christianity. You can admire the Amish for all sorts of things, but for them the important fact is that they are Christians. They live together as a Christian community, and their way of life derives from their understanding of the teachings in the Bible.

At an earlier time in our lives we would probably have skipped over this central fact about the Amish, whom we liked, since it didn't fit in with our perceptions of Christianity, which we saw in a negative light. But now, living for so long in the famished materialism of the booming 1980s, we had become spiritually hungry. We were reaching for God, hoping there was more to life than "dying with the most toys," as the bumper stickers were proclaiming. And we found that God was more than ready to reach for us in return. Reading about the Amish further softened our hearts to religion and made us reconsider Christianity and Jesus. We started reading the sourcebook of the Amish, the Bible, and parts of it began to make sense for the first time. The Bible actually had plenty to say about modern life and how we might reach past the confines of a sick and dying society.

In the winter of 1991, Mary Ann gave birth to our first child, a baby girl. Natasha came into the world at home with a midwife in attendance. This simple event was powerful proof to us that there really were alternatives to the ways of modern life, and that some, at least, were *better*. We had learned what the Amish already knew: that a home birth for a healthy, low-risk mother and child was as safe or safer than a hospital birth according to outcome measures of infant and mother health. The Amish knew it because they made it their business to evaluate everything from the perspective of the well-being of their women, their children, and their communities. Something else that they knew: Home birth is also completely different from medical birth, as we ourselves discovered with the birth of Natasha. In our quiet bedroom, far from the bright lights and electronic noise of the hospital maternity ward, there was a clear experience of the presence of God there with us. Outside the mechanistic, problem-oriented routines of medical birth, we discovered that birth is *holy*. We'd merely hoped for a safe, natural birth, but we received the gift of a supernatural experience as an added measure.

What we had learned from the Amish spurred us to read about the other plain congregations that originated in sixteenth-century Europe: the German Brethren, the Swiss Mennonites, and the Hutterites (known collectively as Anabaptists). Tucked onto the same set of library shelves were books about the Society of Friends, although the Friends themselves originated in another century and in a different place. The Society of Friends, with no prior connection to the Anabaptists, paralleled their development and shared many of their beliefs, even experiencing the same kind of church- and state-sponsored persecution.

The Friends came to exist during a period of intense social confusion in England during the mid-1600s. It was the only sect among the throng of new and extreme Christian groups that formed during that time to survive, becoming a large and dynamic assembly in both England and the American colonies. Early Friends were subject to unrelenting harassment by church authorities and local magistrates, and many died in prison.

Anabaptists and Quakers shared a number of beliefs that made them intolerable to the existing order. Both stressed that only adults making a conscious choice could become Christians—one couldn't inherit the kingdom of heaven through infant baptism or merely by being born into a family of church members. They agreed that our daily lives as committed believers should reflect God's kingdom, "on earth as it is in heaven," which meant in effect that every day was Sunday. Being in loving communion with one another, loving our enemies and refusing to make war, not honoring people of higher rank with special titles or exaggerated shows of respect—all of these stances were contrary to the powers in Europe and England, and resulted in much suffering for both Quakers and Anabaptists.

It is no wonder that both sects emphasized their separateness from the sinful oppression around them by adopting plain, unadorned habits of dress and speech.

There were, however, some important differences between the English and European plain sects. The Anabaptists held to Martin Luther's Reformation dictum of "Scripture alone" wherever Church tradition had run counter to the Gospel. But Friends did not accept that formulation any more than they did the Counter-Reformation's call to "tradition alone." Instead, the founder of the Friends, George Fox, and his followers recognized God's *Spirit* as the guiding authority for Christians. The Author of the

Scriptures could also speak directly to our condition and shape our traditions. With fellow believers and the Bible as reference points, we could go inward and listen for God's divine leadings in our hearts. Worship, ministry, repentance, and salvation all depended on the direct saving work of Christ in our hearts. Fox agreed with Luther that the Bible was an authoritative correction and reproof to the excesses of the establishment churches, but his understanding of the Holy Spirit's presence and power was much more radical. Fox was proclaiming that "Jesus Christ has come to teach His people, Himself," minute by minute, day by day, in all things, even unto the reading and understanding of the truth in Scripture.

Of course, we only knew all this from books I brought home to read in between tending to the new baby. Mary Ann had chosen to stay home with Natasha, and we found it necessary to emulate the Quakers and Amish a little by simplifying our lives to match the decrease in money. We made our meals from scratch, sold our second car, dressed in inexpensive and more modest clothing.

When we learned of a mainstream Friends meeting nearby, we began attending it for weekly worship. What we had read was written long ago and didn't always resemble what we found in the "liberal" wing of the Quakers. Most of the powerful ministry we received still came primarily from the printed words of Friends who had witnessed to others in previous centuries. They were prolific publishers of what they referred to as Truth with a capital *T*. The individual diary or journal was an especially common vehicle for stories of spiritual uplift and encounter. George Fox's

Journal and that of the American Friend John Woolman are still known today.

Reaching back into a time long ago in which people defied the world to follow a spiritual vision was somehow helping Mary Ann and me in the present to come unstuck from modern society. But in our new, floating, stateless condition, we saw that it was necessary to find others with whom we could be anchored in community, like the Amish and the early Quakers. That was when we sought out the conservative Friends we had occasionally heard tell of in our meeting.

We knew we had a long way to go in learning how to be part of any community—neither of us had ever lived in such a way—and that we would have to pick up everything, from the practice of the Golden Rule to the basic skills of simple living. We could learn a lot more from the Quakers and Amish themselves than we had so far learned from books about them.

Along with beginning to attend meetings in Seth's group of Friends, we also made contacts among the Amish nearest to where we lived, and even started a small magazine called *Plain*, written by and about plain people and eventually made by hand: five thousand copies printed by hand and solar power on an antique press, the pages composed in hand-set type and woodblock illustrations. I became *Plain*'s editor, and with my small salary we were able to move to a neighborhood populated entirely by Amish families in Holmes County, Ohio. There we began our first real lessons in what community is all about.

We rented a house without electricity, complete with a

barn, near the town of Sugarcreek, planning to stay about a year while we simultaneously looked for a permanent home in the Friends community at Barnesville, Ohio. We hoped the year spent in Sugarcreek would teach us how to make our future residence in Barnesville into a self-sufficient homestead.

Although up to that point Mary Ann and I knew little about living off the land, we quickly picked up some useful skills. In the fall, when the grapes on the arbor had ripened sufficiently, our landlady, an older, crisply attired, and severe Amish matron, came by to pick some of them and thoroughly advised Mary Ann on how to can grape juice.

"It's not difficult," she insisted. "Wash the grapes, put two cups in a quart jar, add a quarter cup sugar, and pour on boiling water till the jar's full. Put on the lid, screw on the sealing ring, and boil it in your canner for twenty minutes. You can strain off the seeds and skin when you open the jar to use it. Easy!" We just nodded as she stalked off, evaluating my inexpert hedge trimming with a sadly reproving eye.

"I'm leaving out the sugar," Mary Ann, the natural-foods buff, whispered to me as our canning instructor marched over to the buggy where her husband was waiting patiently to take her home. (When we gave some of the finished juice a few weeks later to some Amish friends, the wife took a sip, and with a concerned look offered that maybe Mary Ann had forgotten to put in the sweetener.)

Little by little we learned how to preserve the harvest and can food in ever greater quantities, until we began to fill the fallow shelves of the fruit cellar in the basement. We learned how to take care of animals that weren't just pets, and how to provide for them with hay and feed I stocked into the loft above the stable. With the extensive help of our Amish friends and neighbors, we learned the use of horse and buggy to get around.

Observing and interacting with the Amish, we came to see that community wasn't just our personal interest or ideal, something we could will into being, like a hobby; it was a human necessity, a natural, structurally implicit part of life for every individual, though they might not yet know it. This kind of community didn't exist at all if it only existed in one's mind, as for example in a computer-driven "virtual community." The community we had discovered was concrete rather than abstract, an actual place with actual people who together were doing the real work of living.

Unlike pretend or fantasy communities, the real one we were learning from wasn't filled with folks hand-picked for their similarities. They did not necessarily really, really *like* one another, nor completely share the same interests. On the contrary, we witnessed a certain bland forbearance between some of the families up and down our road. I never heard one church member utter a discouraging word about another, but it was sometimes the case that I could almost imagine one or another thinking, It's a good thing you're my brother in the church and I have to love you, because I don't especially like you!

These same families helped one another on a daily basis, sharing the work of harvest, building barns and chicken coops and houses together, the women quilting and canning together through the summer months. It wasn't *like* that held this community together. It was *love*.

We learned these lessons mostly from the outside looking in. This was closer than reading books, but we weren't there yet. We did not share in the total commitment our neighbors had made to one another, although we, too, were always treated with loving kindness. They often appeared without prior notice at our door with an offer to join in a yard sale up the road, or with a recipe for Mary Ann. We, in turn, offered the use of our telephone, and Mary Ann passed on some vegetarian recipes some of our neighbors found very curious and interesting. Always there were respectful questions back and forth about our religious beliefs.

We formed lasting friendships with a nearby couple who came for long suppertime conversations while their children played outside with Tasha and Jack. There were invitations to local worship, which we accepted on rare occasions, but even so, Mary Ann and I always knew we were headed to another place, to be among a similar yet different group of people. Our faith community was the Society of Friends.

And so our little family—now five of us, with the birth of baby Susanna, the well-loved sister of three-year-old Jack and five-year-old Tasha—prepared to join the Friends community near Barnesville. At the same time I was organizing an event called the Second Luddite Congress, a sort of ongoing forum on technology and modern life that was going to have its opening session at the big Friends meetinghouse in Barnesville. The success and feedback we were getting from *Plain* magazine made it clear we needed to gather people together to discuss these issues. Ironically, I had to indulge in a greater amount of modern technology than usual in order to pull the congress into shape. I rented cars and drove them back and forth between Sugarcreek and Barnesville almost every week in the early spring of 1996.

One good side effect of all that travel was that I was also able to drive around looking at real estate. Soon after the conference I found a place for us to live near the meetinghouse, and by the end of summer we were packed and ready to move to Barnesville.

On a cold, clear New Year's Day in the winter that followed our move, I was fighting to keep my balance at the top of a tall ladder, half of me on it and half in the branches of the old buckeye tree next to the barn. The barn sits on the ridge top above our Barnesville home, and as I swayed in and out of the tree limbs I caught intermittent glimpses of the hills and valleys spread below me like a snow-covered map of Appalachia. I was in the buckeye looking for a suitable branch from which to make a walking stick. I needed a walking stick because I intended to walk to the state capital and give back my driver's license to the government.

A year before we moved to Barnesville, I had sent my last car to the recyclers, and not owned another since. This created a lot of initial difficulties for Mary Ann and me in Sugarcreek, although we eventually made the transition to horse-and-buggy culture. We had also found ourselves, both in Sugarcreek and now in Barnesville, renting cars on a regular basis to make longer trips. There were other ways to travel to places farther away than a horse could take us, but they involved relying on the help of others—and it was easier to pay money to rent a car than to need other people.

But this arrangement made me feel untrue to myself. It seemed as if we could live a plain life, but only up to the point of needing the support of our community. At that point we switched our standards, and with the rental car we could momentarily return to our old way of living. This weighed more on me than on Mary Ann, who is an inveterate homebody and seldom wishes or needs to journey beyond the borders of the township. I was a lot more of a roamer by nature. As a young man, I had hitchhiked up and down the state on my way to and from the three colleges I drifted in and out of as an unsuccessful, undisciplined student. I got serious about school when I attended an upper-division university in Florida, but I still roamed more or less constantly, now in an old VW that buzzed back and forth between my haunts in and around Miami and the homes of my old hipster friends in Cleveland, traveling as often as every fortnight.

Now, even without actually owning a car, I still was caught up in the life of always being on the road. It had become more important than ever after we moved to Barnesville that I minimize my leavetaking; I wanted to learn to stay put in one place now, to become more and more rooted with my family, our homestead, and our church community. My relationship with the automobile needed further change, because it continued to pose a danger to the notion of coming to rest, of staying in one place.

The ladder teetered and then actually began to slide away from my feet before I hooked it with an ankle and brought it back underneath me. I had just been wondering how many days it might take for me to reach the Ohio capital on foot, given that it was well over a hundred miles.

This wasn't a protest march I was planning—I had no intention of telling more than the necessary few people about it in advance, let alone involving the media. I wasn't going to hold a rally or cause any ruckus once I got to my destination. For me, the trip had come as a Quaker "leading," a necessary thing blossoming in my heart as a directive from God.

In talking over this leading with Seth and another Friend, I had found myself describing it as a needed step in pulling away from the freedom and mobility many people hold up as great achievements of modern life. I had come to see the car and what it represented as paradoxically oppressive, not only to myself, but also to the larger society that had embraced it and the planet that was choking on its fumes. These Friends were both firmly wedded to their automobiles, but they could sympathize with the leading and support it.

" 'The earth is the Lord's, and the fullness thereof,' " Seth had noted one time. "We'll be answering some tough questions one day for wasting and polluting the creation."

Natasha and Jack were below me in the cold fresh air of New Year's morning, circling the buckeye tree with all sorts of shouted questions about walking to Columbus and why Daddy needed to climb a tree to do it. Looking down from my unsteady aspect, I reminded them that Daddy doesn't like to answer questions while doing something dangerous.

I carefully began to saw into the chosen limb, and suddenly inhaled the intense skunk odor that buckeye wood exudes when cut. Breathing it in along with the cold misted air around my head somehow associated the strong smell with my growing resolve to make the envisioned hike. As soon as the branch was free I turned my attention to the problem of getting down the ladder with the saw and unwieldy branch held together under one arm.

Mary Ann and I don't spend New Year's Eve in drunken revelry, so Mom and Dad are always in good shape on New Year's Day, ready to do some special things with the children. Because there's no television, we have plenty of time for fun together; there aren't any "special" programs or sporting events on the tube to keep us from having a real day, spent as a family. And so New Year's has become an important occasion for us.

We use part of the day to plan for spring, a very pleasant task in the middle of an Ohio winter. The wood furnace works away to keep us warm as we gather around the big cherrywood table in the dining room, and someone lights the double gas lamp above it, even though it's the middle of the day. Tomatoes from the harvest stew on the stove, steaming the air with the smell of last summer's canning sessions.

We began by discussing the layout of the new gardens

we'll be plowing up in the yard come spring. Jack, who this year had made a transition from cherubic blond toddler to burly he-man, liked to confide to everyone who would listen that he wanted to be a trash hauler when he grows up. This aspiration, however, had started to fade now that his mother was giving nightly readings aloud from *Farmer Boy*. On this New Year's Day he was all Almanzo Wilder, garden-planting farmer boy. He puffed out his chest and threw back his head in a show of self-importance, at which I joked he would make a more stalwart horse to hitch to a garden plow than would Ned, our nervous standardbred. This he took as a compliment. Leaning over my sketch of our new homestead and tentative placement of garden plots, he bellowed out the song of the animals from the previous chapter book Mom had read to him, *Rabbit Hill*:

NEW FOLKS COMIN',
OH MY!
NEW FOLKS COMIN', OH MY!

(I had been trying all autumn and winter—so far without success—to teach Jack not to shout each and every thing he wanted to communicate.)

Jack wanted to know whether we would share our new garden with the wild animals. As I worked on the garden map he kept reminding me about the generous New Folks of Rabbit Hill and their garden statue of Saint Francis that bore the legend, "There is enough for all." Perhaps I should look through my garden fencing catalog some other time, I thought. (I'd ordered it on the advice of our neighbor two doors down, who told me the raccoons around here think there is only enough sweet corn for them.)

Tasha's approach to the garden planning was more serious than that of her little brother. Just as willowy and sensitive in manner as Jack was solid and apparently thick-skinned, Tasha was nevertheless a girl with some backbone to her, and she considered herself the children's advocate in matters of family business. Not quite six years old, she was already a gifted first-grader in Mom's home school. She read a few grades above her level and had mastered enough of her *Ray's Arithmetic* (published in the 1800s, when math textbooks meant their business) to already be totaling up the dimensions of the area set aside for the new children's garden.

"Is that going to be big enough?" she asked doubtfully.

Smacking the table with her hands, two-year-old Susanna gave us learned, unintelligible gardening advice from her straitjacketed position in the high chair. I handed her a duplicate seed catalog to demolish as the rest of us pored over pictures of Luther Hill sweet corn and Nantes carrots, bush pinto beans and Long Pie pumpkins, Kennebec potatoes and Amish Paste tomatoes. Mary Ann in particular wanted to try lots of things this first gardening year to see what would do well in the sandy Appalachian soil.

The older children went off by themselves for a while to come up with a written plan and a picture of their own garden—a little of everything, as it turned out, but especially lots of lettuce (perhaps to feed the wild rabbit population?). They hoped their garden would produce vegetables they could sell themselves at the local farmers' market in the summer, providing a little money for birthday and Christmas presents.

This year we also made a bird calendar, much like the one hanging in the kitchen of our Amish friends David and Elsie. All our family members old enough to hold a crayon without eating it drew bird pictures around the border on a large creamy yellow sheet of paper. Tasha filled the interior with numbered lines. Throughout the winter and on until next New Year's, we would note down on the numbered lines the name of each kind of bird that flew over our land or the pasture below us. In the months since our move we had already spied bluebirds, yellow finches, and mourning doves along the fence row. Wintertime had brought boxing matches between a heavyweight team of cardinals and an equally well-developed pair of blue jays, all rounds being conducted in the vicinity of the feeder hanging from the magnolia tree.

Earlier I had brought in the buckeye branch and left it in the basement to dry for a few weeks before I stripped off the bark. Upstairs, the children went back outside to play while Mary Ann and I once again sat together at the big table and talked about my walk to Columbus.

"I can go after the garden is plowed, but before we plant the late crops," I suggested by way of homing in on a departure date in early spring.

"But what if something happens to you on the road? Scott, it's not as safe as it was when you were hitchhiking around in your teens!"

(If only she knew how "safe" that had been. Flashing across my memory was an episode where I unwittingly hopped into the backseat of an old Mustang full of green smoke, my legs instantly buried up to the knees in empty beer cans, two inebriated faces leering back at me through the haze—"Sowhere yagoin, man?" It was a weird era, and I was a different person.)

"Well, I won't be hitchhiking. I'm walking. And besides, I'll be reciting the first part of the Sermon on the Mount while I walk; I want to commit the beatitudes to memory. Whatever happens, the Lord will still be with me."

"But you will call, won't you, every day? In case something happens or there's an emergency."

She was feeling anxious for me—and for herself and the children—at the thought of a week's separation. But Mary Ann is a Friend, and I knew she did not want to give in to fear and stand in the way of a leading, a spiritual command from God. The journey from modern to plain living had often called for her to yield to the Divine will, and she had learned to honor and follow that Inward Guide. That is what set her and other Friends apart as a religious people. Not only were they to listen for the Lord's commands, they were to follow them:

"Ye are my friends, if ye do whatsoever I command you."

Already her natural fear of the unknown was being replaced by questions of a practical nature. She would have to do my chores while I was gone, feeding the horse and the other animals up at the barn, and take on some of the routines of self-sufficiency I had been doing, such as periodically checking the cistern and pumping water up to it from the well if it was low.

We were expecting another baby—not until midsummer, but there was no telling what her energy level would be come spring. Mary Ann is an independent woman in many ways, and I would have to pick the right time to suggest that some of the women in our community should come by to give her a hand while I was away.

Our conversation turned to the children, how my time away might affect them. Most parents today, I suppose, would not consider the absence of one adult for a week or two harmful or even noteworthy. But our children didn't have the sort of independent lives that have become common for modern kids, who are transferred daily from home to day care or school and on to organized activities and entertainments, in the care of a succession of adults.

Our children are at home mostly, where Mom is a sure and continuous presence, and where Daddy returns in the late afternoon on most days to spend time working and playing with them. At the end of the day I'm often there in the rocker, little one on my knee, while the others curl up with Mom on the couch for the evening chapter-book reading. I'm not a superdad, and sometimes I'm not there when I ought to be, but for Tasha, Jack, and Susanna it would be very different indeed without me there.

I decided to make a simple map of my route for them, divided into each day's journey so that they would know approximately where I was on a given day. I would tape it to the dining room wall before I left.

Having made our plans for spring, played a bit, and read more of Almanzo's adventures, we popped some corn on the kitchen stove and sat around the cherry table once more to play a slightly inane board game—the Bird Game, as a favor to Jack, who found it bracingly challenging—still thinking and talking about the gardens of summers to come.

Soon Susanna was back up in the rocker hearing her favorite bedtime story about Nicholas, a little bunny who enjoys nature all the year round, and who, when winter comes, curls up inside his warm little hollow tree and dreams about spring.

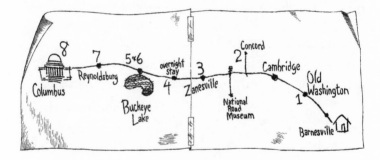

The First Day

Blessed are the poor in spirit: for theirs is the kingdom of heaven.

When the snowy day in early Fourth Month* finally arrives, I am up early and ready for the journey. I have my buckeye walking stick in hand; more of a staff than a cane, it comes up to my shoulder. There is a bend in it just at hand height, and the nob at the top still has its rough bark to provide some grip should I need to lean on it. Otherwise it is sanded smooth and varnished, though it still has a slight odor of skunk about it. I have tried it out on some conditioning hikes over a few miles and find it a helpful bit of technology, the only walking tool I'll need besides a pair of shoes.

In our region of Appalachia it seems that the concept of a level berm of gravel alongside the road has never been

---

*Conservative Friends use the numbers for the names of the months and days of the week instead of the common, mostly pagan-derived names.

entertained by our transportation officials. As a result of this lapse in thinking, most rights-of-way simply drop off to a ditch where the asphalt ends. Sometimes they drop off to nothing, and the roadside walker is in danger not only of twisting an ankle in a rut off the pavement, but of actually tumbling down the mountainside. With cars and pickup trucks blasting past me along the state thoroughfare, I learned that the wooden staff I was holding could be stuck down into whatever was next to the road, and thus would help me balance on the pavement's edge, saving me from either being flattened or disappearing into the hollow below.

Snow fell last night; it is about twenty-five degrees outside as the sun comes up. I was ready for this and am dressed in several layers of plain garb, including a black coat with hook-and-eye fastenings and a notched stand-up collar (I bought the coat from an Amish clothier; a Quaker would think that simple black buttons were unadorned enough). I'm also wearing a black cotton sweatshirt and my rather battered around-the-farm broad-brimmed felt hat. If it stays this cold, I'll trade the hat for a warmer ski mask in my pack.

Inside the pack I also have a few changes of underwear and socks, a little food, a compass, water, my straw hat for warmer weather, a Bible. Laminated map sections the size of my hand are clipped together on the side of the canvas pack. In my coat pocket there is an old Friends Tract Society printing of the Sermon on the Mount. And, of course, my driver's license.

The children are silently huddled together on the cold

kitchen floor by the back door. Tasha hands me my stick; her jaw is set, as it is when she's willing herself to calmness—a facade of dignified nonchalance that can't possibly hold through the day. Her mother's going to have a time with her later today, I would guess.

Jack's usually fake courage seems more genuine this morning, as he neither cries nor acts up. He just gives some quiet goodbye hugs and holds little Susanna's hand up to make it wave as I head out the door. Temporarily pulled back inside by a hand on my shoulder, I find myself in a last embrace with Mary Ann.

The barn at the top of the hill is warm inside. I love the quiet here and the smell of straw and hay. It's a pleasure to pour water into the various drinking containers of the animals. Ned, my driving horse, is waiting impatiently by the feed box in his stall. He almost knocks the grain scoop out of my hands trying to nose into the stream of oats as I give him his daily ration. Ned is what horse people call a "poor keeper," meaning that much of the grain he takes into his mouth dribbles right back out and onto the stall floor. Today I note that some of these wayward oat seeds have taken root and sprouted in the dirt under and around the feed box. I give him an extra scoop in the hope that he'll keep more of it where it's supposed to be.

My first destination today is the office of *Plain*. The office is near the Friends meetinghouse, and it only takes a short while to walk there. Loren, *Plain*'s typesetter and secretary, has come in early so we can discuss what work needs to be done while I'm away. There is a wide brick path that leads to the meetinghouse, and I head there after our conversation, intending the porch of the meetinghouse to be the starting point of my trip. God willing, I won't stop until I'm standing under the statehouse dome in Columbus.

Now there are some quiet moments on a bench on the porch.

Then I'm up and on my way.

The sun shines on the previous night's covering of snow. It feels quite exciting to be leaving. It's also very cold, and I sing to keep warm. The song is specially chosen, a final factor of planning for the trip, something we worked out yesterday during our time of devotion together as a family.

Every morning the five of us regather around the table after breakfast for some Bible reading, prayers for those who need them, and a spontaneously chosen song or hymn that we sing together. (It's not always as spontaneous as it could be. Every day Jack asks us to pray for Tony in England, who's been ill for a long time, and Susanna blurts out her eternally unchanging song request for "The Wise Man Built His House upon the Rock".) Yesterday we picked songs in advance to be sung each morning in devotion time, so that we might share in our daily worship though we are far apart.

Today's song is a bold and happy hand-clapping rendition of Isaiah, the twelfth verse of the fifty-fifth chapter:

> You shall go out with joy
> and be brought forth in peace!
> The mountains and the hills

shall break forth before you!
There'll be shouts of joy
and all the trees of the field
will clap, will clap their hands!

Well, *that's* a good way to start, very brave. To walk
to Columbus, all I need to do is make it to the village of
Barnesville . . . and then hike another hundred-plus miles
west. Today's plan is to take a back road northwest out
of the village that will get me up to state Route 40, formerly U.S. 40, formerly the National Road. I can pick up
Route 40 tomorrow from today's destination, the town of
Old Washington.

It seems to have started out well enough, although I
feel a little self-conscious walking along the sidewalk in
Barnesville with my staff. An unnecessary and overly ro-
mantic affectation, I fear. I should have left it at home.
Suddenly the whole idea seems singularly stupid. Why do
I need to walk to another city to ditch my license and
memorize some Bible verses? Why have I made myself
vulnerable and risked a whole slew of potential dangers
just to make some point to myself?

Maybe it *is* foolish to act on our prompting from the
Holy Spirit if we act in a foolish way, like carrying this
ridiculous stick, wearing this funny-looking hat. On the
other hand, I know I am being led—I *believe,* and in my
belief I have heard the Lord speak to my condition and my
concern. Put into my heart was the decision to go forward
on this trip. Maybe my methods are flawed or even laugh-
able, but I believe . . . and here I am.

All the doubt and shame roll through me like a rainstorm and are gone. Yes, I'm silly, but look how free, how *good* it feels to trust a leading from God. I admit this is a strange thing I am doing, and even I don't fully understand it. The mystery of it makes it all the more exciting; God must have some important surprises in store for me along the way.

Padding down the sidewalk toward the two- and three-story facades of the Barnesville business district, I continue to feel a bit self-conscious. I push my staff through a loop at the back of my pack so that it less conspicuously hangs behind me.

Across from the Starfire gas station the local newspaper office anchors the central district. Bruce, the former editor, was an important player in the restoration of the main block of stores. You used to be able to see him afternoons writing copy in his cubbyhole office back behind the typing pool. After years of harried deadline catching with his tiny staff of five, he decided a few months ago to accept an offer with an urban renewal program in Columbus. I'm sorry he's gone. I treasure the friends I've made in my growing familiarity with this place.

Having spent my life moving from town to town, often living in suburbs where there is no "there," no center at all, it makes me happy to think I might at last be putting roots beneath me. I feel that, at the least, there is a developing camaraderie with some of the people behind the storefronts. Crossing the street again and moving past the big mom-and-pop video store, I continue westward on Main Street. The door to the Good News bookstore is open, and

Michele waves to me from where she is restocking the glass jars along the candy counter. When Michele and her husband, Steve, took over the store they had the lottery machine removed, so now the after-school candy buyers are an important replacement source of income. A few steps farther on, Bill the accountant smiles and nods from behind the curtains and plate glass of his perfectly maintained storefront. Bill and his wife run an independent one-room Christian elementary school on the meetinghouse grounds.

Only a few pedestrians are around this weekday morning, walking past what appear to be rich and varied edifices of commerce. But there really isn't much commerce going on here. What shops exist serve a loyal but often dwindling clientele. A Wal-Mart and three or four other "box" stores are only twenty miles away, across from the mall that killed business here in Barnesville twenty-five years ago. Now the mall is itself being strangled by the boxes.

The upper windows of the buildings in the business district here are not painted with the names of tax consultants, lawyers, land speculators, or all the other hoped-for tenants when these thousands upon thousands of square feet of space were constructed in the late 1800s. Although most of the windows on the upper floors are either blank or shuttered today, I doubt the spaces above me were ever completely filled. A lot of small towns overbuilt during that time of easy credit from poorly regulated banks. There was a bank panic at the end of the century that froze these buildings at the moment of their economic undoing.

When Mary Ann and I lived in northeastern Ohio, we

began to investigate the towns near where I grew up, in the area of Middlefield and Burton, and the local economy of the nearby Amish. It was another economy frozen in time, but unlike Barnesville's, it was prosperous and alive. Just as we try to buy locally now that we live in Barnesville—such as the walking shoes I'm wearing this morning, which I purchased right in the next block of stores—we began to buy locally in the Amish area of Middlefield, especially our footwear.

One time, on a dreary autumn morning, Tasha (then three and a half) and I were to be found squeezing our way between several cars and black buggies filling the parking lot of Yoder's shoe shop, a mile outside Middlefield village. As we entered the warmly lit interior, Tasha gave a little hop of excitement, because we were there that day to buy some shoes and a pair of boots for her. I was pleased, too, because I was dropping off my sturdy and plain high-topped shoes for repair—repair instead of replacement would save money for our family. I had purchased them from Mr. Yoder almost two years before. The previous winter he'd resoled them and added a heel cleat to help them wear less quickly.

Tasha knew this store well. Paying no attention to the tall shelves of neatly arranged shoe and boot boxes, she wended her way through the narrow aisles. Miscellaneous horse tack was hanging from the ceiling, along with the two pressurized kerosene lamps that were burning that morning. Lamp supplies covered a divider wall; on the other side of it were rows of men's hats and socks. Tasha turned to the right and found the little corner by the woodstove where two chairs sat directly across from a large, glass-fronted case. In the case were samples of the styles of shoes available, all closely arranged on three shelves.

As you might guess, all the footwear at Yoder's, from jogging shoes to work boots, is black. This is in violation of one of the two major promises with which chain stores seduce us: unlimited selection. The other promise, service (which, in large stores, is actually intrusive promotion and salesmanship) was equally lacking at Yoder's. The few chairs were already filled with two families' children, but no one, least of all the shopkeeper, seemed to be in anything like a frantic hurry—as indeed, neither were we.

Whether it was the God-centeredness of their lives (a point of view that tends to focus on the eternal rather than the ephemeral) or the bequeathed life skills of Amish culture, which make it seem as if everyone in their society knows what they're doing, knows what's expected, knows what comes next—whatever the reason, walking into Yoder's had the effect of making time slow nearly to a standstill.

Seeing there were no seats, Tasha turned right around and headed back toward the entrance where we had already noticed a nice pair of snowboots (black) displayed on the end of a shelf.

She knew this store so well because for most of her three and a half years it had been the only place we'd purchased footwear, as was probably true for most of the Amish living within driving distance. It was our pleasure to do so. Shopping in the local economy was returning money to people—not businesses so much as *people*—whom we wanted to be there for a long time. It was a commitment: If I wanted Yoder's to be there in the future, I couldn't go to Wal-Mart to buy Tasha's boots on sale. In the way of accounting that the Amish were unknowingly teaching us, it would simply cost too much to save that little bit of money.

Yoder's is a single link in a local economy of Amish home-based businesses stretching over three or four townships. They include five bakeries, two blacksmiths, three bookstores, four buggy shops, two bulk food stores, ten cabinetmakers, two engine repair shops, two fabric stores, four harness makers, five general stores, five greenhouses, a hardware store, four maple-syrup-producing sugarbushes, a retail sales orchard, four quilt shops, a saw shop, a sewing machine repair shop, two window and siding contractors, and six wood-products (lawn furniture, toys) businesses, plus countless roadside produce stands and the family farming operations that are many times more numerous than nonfarming businesses (and often exist alongside them).

Most of these establishments are successful and have been around for a long time. They are geographically arranged so that none competes directly with any other for business.

Since most Americans now hear a steady barrage of propaganda about the global economy, it is a blessing to have experienced these places within the Amish local economy. Amish society is itself a blessing simply because it exists. It is the bumblebee that experts tell us is aerodynamically unsuited for flight. But the bumblebee does fly, and the supremely nonglobal Amish economy is a living example that does work. We can point to it when we're told that there can be no returning to the dark, deprived days of the local economy. The Amish version is quite similar to what was standard in the Midwest of the last century. The truth is that the Amish haven't developed some strange and completely new system—the modern experts and economists have.

The unchanging quality of Amish life gives us a chance to compare and see if we really are better off competing in the global economy. My experiences in Middlefield, and later in the even larger Amish community in Holmes County, Ohio, lead me to believe that if you could participate in this joyous reminder of what we once had, you would want to know how we let good places like Barnesville fall into economic disrepair.

As Tasha sat on the counter that morning I paid friend Yoder for the new shoes (same model as the previous year, but Tasha was still excited—she'd never been exposed to all the latest movie tie-in apparel at the mall, didn't know or care about Barbie or the Little Mermaid) and the snow-boots. He explained to me that he had so much repair business that it might be months before he could completely resole my plain black boots. The last time it had taken a few weeks. Electing simply to replace the heels this time, I asked him whether the new discount boot store in town was taking away customers. He practically snorted at the question, his expression saying, I wish it would. But his more Amish-like reply was a low-key "Not so's you'd notice."

I didn't doubt him. There had been, by my count, ten

or more customers through the store in the half hour we'd spent there.

What exactly makes Yoder's different from the apparel store in Barnesville that is barely hanging on, the one whose awning I'm passing under right now? Many of the newer businesses here are run by cheerful evangelical Christians who seem eager to please their customers, but the apparel stores are part of an old guard. When I bought the shoes for my walk to Columbus from one of them, I found it a depressing experience. The owners seemed re-signed to their impending fate. Their store is mostly empty of customers, and the salesclerks spend much of the day drinking coffee at Patrick's Restaurant down on the corner, rather than racking their brains for better ways to offer their wares or meet their customers' needs, as some of the spiritually motivated newer shopkeepers have done. But who can really say why they are failing?

It is on this spiritual plane that the Amish shopkeepers have to operate within their own communities. They have problems, too, of course. They have their share of horse traders who drive an aggressive bargain to the point that would make a Quaker blush—but we can recognize these lapses without losing sight of their overall success at main-taining morality and servanthood as values in their dealings.

Another factor is that the Amish, and to a lesser extent some groups of Friends, live in genuine communities, and they support one another. They also restrain one another, as they are required to live up to the community's standards.

Even with these human-imposed behaviors, I still think the Amish would fail to repel the global economy if they weren't seeking God's help to overcome the daily temptations of greed, competition, and the easy dollar. It is this sense of humility that lifts us from the corruption and brings us into lasting right relations with one another. In today's economic system, the only real solution for a place like Barnesville is to put ourselves under the Golden Rule.

In my memory, Tasha carries her little box of shoes out of the store, walking happily under the hissing lamps. It is true that the shoes themselves were not locally made, having been produced several hundred miles away in a factory, but as we rode away that day I couldn't help but hope that someday Tasha will be able to buy shoes for her children that are made locally, from local materials, by someone who cares about what they're doing.

I have made it as far as the main intersection in Barnesville, one of the five traffic lights in town. Looking across the street, I notice with a start and then a sinking feeling that the old variety store on the corner, the last large retailer downtown, has hung a huge orange-and-blue GOING OUT OF BUSINESS sign across the broad plate-glass exterior. Others walking by are turning to look at the big sign, too.

Another store will probably settle into its place, as it took the place of a previous department store on that site. I have to remind myself that the entire village isn't falling apart. There's a new library a few blocks behind me, thoughtfully erected downtown instead of out by the fast-food places on the eastern edge. Jeff, the librarian, is involved in the resurgence of civic pride and restoration that has come in the last few decades.

What is happening here economically, though, is a slow-motion vanishing of local commerce, of businesses owned by people instead of by stockholders, to the point where even a variety store can't eke out a living for its owner in a village of four thousand people.

There's no more time to think about it. I'm through the intersection, walking under the Hometown Pizza awning, and on out of the village in short order. Now the view is unfamiliar. This is pretty much unexplored territory for me, a carless Quaker living east of Barnesville.

At the hospital I take what I believe to be the correct turn to the left onto a slim, rocky road that wanders past the township garage. The country here is wild and beautiful. Hundred-year-old maples tower over the tangled bunches of invading multiflora roses that crowd old fences along the road. The rutted gravel plunges down and to the right into the woods. The shadowed morning air is colder here, and I can see my breath again.

It isn't so clear to me now that I am indeed traveling on the right road after all. Looking up at the position of the sun through the trees, I can tell I'm pointed the right way, but the road itself has given way from gravel to big rocks, and finally to dirt. An even smaller lane, not on the map, climbs upward to the left, but I continue down the slope until the road abruptly ends against the edge of a wide streambed.

An hour into my brave little eight-day journey and I am lost. The map holds no explanation for where I am. Having decided to try the smaller lane to the left that I just passed, I start back uphill. Gaining the new lane, I find that a short way up it there is an abandoned farm with a barn and fenced fields overgrown with sumac and heaped-up tangles of multiflora rose. Beyond the farm the road is impassable, covered by massive fallen oaks that have been deliberately hewed down over it.

From up here I can see down to where the bigger road ends at the water's edge, but it actually continues up a hill on the other side of the stream. It goes on into a field, still traveling in roughly the right direction. Above it on a far hillside there is a large and beautiful white barn caught in the late morning light. Along the broader of the two sides that I can see are four low windows rimmed in red. On the narrower side facing the valley into which the road disappears are nine red-shuttered openings arranged up its towering white wall.

I decide to take a shortcut down the hill to the stream, with the intention of fording it at a narrower place I've spied. I slip, and there is a scary moment when I am sliding out of control down the broken rocks that cover the hill. A familiar pinch inside my knee tells me it's out of whack now.

Not just lost, but also somewhat lame. Today's song seems ever more premature. The staff turns out to be a very necessary affectation at this point, giving my aching knee some support and assertively guiding me from stone to stone across the water. Slowly clambering up the steep grade on the other side, I feel a little more optimistic again.

Once on the new section of gravel road, I begin to notice a change coming over this part of the woodland, more noticeable the higher I climb: Farther out from the tall maples and oaks that grow along the sides of the main road (off to my right I can still hear cars speeding by), the trees and underbrush and pasture give way to a scraped-clean wasteland that stretches ahead and all around for several miles. The coal company has stripped and ripped everything apart into a moonscape. I've been walking on an abandoned coal-hauling road all this time! By accident I've found the backstage reality of my rural home, a blasted place normally hidden from us by a line of trees.

Still drinking in the sheer barrenness of it all, my thoughts turn back to town and the renovated streets and sidewalks, the repointed granite block work and brick facades. An hour ago I was admiring the antique shape of the new streetlights—a preservationist's dream, really—lighting the nearly empty sidewalk of an economically hollowed-out rural village.

And here the land has been wasted for the coal that fires the power plants of Appalachia. The streetlights are plugged into that power, which sends its waste sulfur all the way to the Adirondacks.

The beautiful white barn is still visible from my plateau, high on a ridge to the north. But there's no more road to follow, and I must turn around and hike back down and across the stream. Eventually I gain the main road again and follow it a few more miles, looking for my turn.

It's been several hours and I'm barely away from Barnesville. Putting my hand into my inner coat pocket, I draw out the Sermon on the Mount that I had planned to memorize on this trip. I don't feel much like memorizing just now; truthfully, I can't remember why I wanted to commit the beatitudes to memory in the first place. But here's the first one:

"Blessed are the poor in spirit:
for theirs is the kingdom of heaven."

The New English Bible translation, which often seems a little more precise than the King James, both expands and contracts this saying of Jesus:

"How blest are those who know that they are poor;
the kingdom of Heaven is theirs."

The meaning here is that the poor in spirit are those who know they can do nothing without God. The poor in spirit know, through either experience or revelation, that we really can't forge our own destiny or make our own way through the world, at least not without great suffering and failure. And those who know this about themselves are also most open to God's saving grace through Jesus. Giving up the self to God, we do His perfect will, here on earth as it is in heaven.

William Barclay, in his famous commentary on the Gospel of Matthew, paraphrases the first of the beatitudes thusly:

O THE BLISS OF THE MAN WHO HAS REALIZED HIS OWN UTTER HELP-LESSNESS, AND WHO HAS PUT HIS WHOLE TRUST IN GOD, FOR THUS

ALONE HE CAN RENDER TO GOD THAT PERFECT OBEDIENCE WHICH WILL MAKE HIM A CITIZEN OF THE KINGDOM OF HEAVEN!

Maybe this would be a good opportunity to memorize it after all. "Blessed are the poor in spirit: for theirs is the kingdom of heaven," I recite, coming around the bend next to a vine-covered abandoned silo. The wood-staved silo sits next to a thoroughly collapsed barn, and I see that a pair of wrinkle-headed turkey buzzards lounge on the silo's jagged rim, presumably a good spot from which to detect roadkill along this stretch of pavement. I feel as if I have begun to see the ruins behind the facade of rural existence; even the facade itself is beginning to thin out and blow away in bits and pieces of decay.

Perhaps this is what we need to know: that there really is no escape from the problems we ourselves have created, neither an escape to wilderness nor an escape to Disney World. We are intimately tied up in nature's reality; if nature has been degraded, then so have we. What we've done can't just be brushed off. It sticks. It is our reflection, and it shows back to us our terrible disconnection from the lessons of limitation and abundance that God has posed to us in His creation.

Here now is the white barn that I spied from the coal wastes. The paint on it is fresh, the facilities inside abandoned only momentarily, until the evening milking. Just ahead at an unmarked crossroad (none of the roads so far have, in fact, had any signs or markings whatsoever), I walk onto the lawn of a farmhouse and pull off my pack to see if my other map is any better than the one I've been consulting. It doesn't much help to consult a map when you don't know where you are on it, or the names of any of the roads you've passed. It does seem like I might be at a place on this map where I should bear to the right, and so I do, pulling the pack up onto my back again and trudging reluctantly up a gravel hill. After two miles on this road it becomes obvious I've made another bad guess. The way has circled back toward Barnesville.

It's noon. Sitting on a hillside, I take out some bread and cheese to give thanks over. Blessed are the poor in spirit. Half the day is gone and I have easily walked eight or ten miles, but I am, in all likelihood, only a mile or two from the edge of the village.

Turning back down the road the way I have come, I hear from over the hillside the sound of someone talking. A coal company man in his American Power pickup truck is chatting on his cell phone. This, too, is a coal road, an active one.

Yes, he knows the way to Pultney Ridge (my intended route), and proceeds to give me some rather vague directions before driving off. I've always considered myself well able to find my way around; I even pride myself on it, to the point where I sometimes tease my wife about her lack of directional sense—and she doesn't like being teased. For all my preparations for the trip, I never gave much consideration to losing my way. I brought a compass along, but that was for a nature hike I'm planning for farther up the road.

At an even more dejected pace I set off again, retracing my steps and then at some point realizing I must have missed Pultney Ridge. At least I'm on a real road and traveling in the right direction. The sun lights and warms the cold air, and I see that the countryside is becoming beautiful and unspoiled again. The walking itself is easy, mostly level or downhill. A good thing, since I still have so far to go today.

Whatever else you could say about my horse, Ned (and I could say plenty—I'll have to describe Ned in detail sometime on this walk), he's a good traveler in terms of endurance. He can easily make a twenty-mile trip in one day, as long as there is a significant rest stop and some water to drink along the way. In that sense he's reliable, having been trained to pace himself at a steady speed. Today I need to remember this good quality of Ned's and emulate it.

Soon after a brief conversation with a passing farmer I come up some hills and find the first really well-kept farm I've seen since leaving the area east of Barnesville. Getting closer, I realize it's an Amish homestead. My random route through the hills has put me in the small Amish settlement north of Quaker City. Crossing the main north-south route, I come across several more houses, all more or less alike in the way that Amish homes are: neat and tidy places rumped into the hillsides, with walk-out basements. Nearby clotheslines are hung with all the laundry since the main washing day of Monday: pastel dresses waving in the cold sunshine and broadfall pants hanging by their flaps. In every case there is a workshop of some size close to the house, a garden, a small horse barn. These Amish, then, do not make their primary cash income from farming, or their livestock facilities would be more imposing. It is likely the men mostly "work out," meaning they work away from home as carpenters and other tradesmen.

The beautiful standardbred horses moving about the fields to graze in their stately fashion remind me of our stay in the area near Sugarcreek, among the Holmes County Amish. Like them, we lived in a neat home without electricity, flanked by a horse barn and pasture. Living there made it apparent that the Amish have a detailed, prepackaged plan for living. Lifestyle in a can. Questions such as "What sort of house design would I like to have?" don't get asked, nor do "Which day of the week am I going to wash clothes?" and "What style of clothes should I wear?" Most of the questions that modern people face about day-to-day living—and solve as matters of personal taste or as expressions of individual personality—have already been decided for an Amish person. This is true to a slightly lesser extent for other plain people.

Within our own Quaker community we have gradually come to realize that even though many daily decisions are already settled for us by our collective, written-down Discipline (unlike the Amish, who pass on instructions orally from one generation to the next), they instigate an uncomfortably wide range of responses in personal behavior these days. The Discipline requires that Friends in good standing wear modest clothing, but in the least conservative meetings First Day worship can be a fashion show. On the other hand, we and a few other families wear totally un-adorned uniforms, beyond the requirements of the Discipline, creating an even more pronounced incongruity with the fancier brethren than if we were to stick to the minimum requirement.

Many of the personal choices Mary Ann and I have made to live free of worldly encumbrances were made before we joined our current meeting. Yet one of the factors that led us to accept the authority of our religious group was the emphasis in the Discipline on the sober use of our time here on earth. Mary Ann and I had already lived without television all of our adult lives when we first read of the Amish people's objection to bringing this unreliable stranger into the home. Their witness went further, however, and they forbade themselves even the "friendlier" stranger of radio. When we looked at how we used radio in our life together as a substitute for other, more direct inter-actions, we, too, decided to turn it out of our house.

Right away I noticed the improvement in my life; at that point in our marriage I was coming home from work and making supper many nights, standing in the kitchen with National Public Radio warbling, stir-frying the rice and snow peas, listening to Mary Ann tell me about her day while I tried to pay attention to our toddler. The confusion and stress of all the input often led to frustration, burnt meals, arguments. Radio, supper, Mary Ann, Tasha—too many stimuli, and one of them had to go! After the radio was given to Goodwill (the choice of victims had been easy), my nightly reentry into home life became much more calm and satisfying. And I could still find out what was going on in the world if I wanted to, by looking at a newspaper.

The Friends' Discipline warns against amusements and entertainments both because they divert us from a constant spiritual consideration of our actions and because they encourage our animal nature, our lower, strictly-of-the-flesh selves. Not a modern concept, to be sure! But the more modern view has crept in for some of our members. We had always assumed there were none in our group who owned televisions, yet it turns out that many do. Like the Bible, the general guidelines of the Discipline are subject to interpretation. People like Seth and myself would rather err on the conservative side, others on the liberal side. The Amish have chosen a route that appears steadier, elevating group interpretation of Scriptural commands above any personal revelation.

I could probably accept the strict conformity to group understanding of God's will (and the resulting lack of choice) better than some who have lived with it all their lives. I'm thinking of those who wish for more freedom than their Amish lifestyle allows, who push against the boundaries. I'm also thinking of some of the lifelong conservative Friends who have tasted that freedom and are bringing a more modern outlook to bear than do the newer, younger converts.

Mary Ann and I now have been in both worlds, the world of submission and the world of self-will, and our experiences and comparisons run counter to what one might expect. For example, back when we were dating, we wanted to make ourselves a good-looking couple. I wanted everyone to see me looking great with this beautiful girl on my arm. But the cult of self was really a more demanding master than is the dress standard of modesty we live by today. To look good—to be fashionable and "sexy"—meant lots of shopping trips and lots of money for clothes and jewelry. Mary Ann was the first to acknowledge how ridiculous and wasteful it was to play the looking-good game. One day she simply decided she wasn't going to wear anything uncomfortably tight or anything that was not chaste and unrevealing. The shopping sprees ended, along with the underlying insecurity caused by focusing on externals. Dressing simply, and then, as a witness to the world, dressing plainly, put us back under an unchanging standard.

The Amish retain a similarly settled worldview that changes little from one generation to the next. Their blueprint for daily conduct is the Bible, unchanging, not subject to revision (though necessarily open to interpretation).

This seems narrow and confining to the modern mind, and is rejected out of hand as a horrible fundamentalist position (read ayatollahlike theocracy, holy war, suppression of human rights—all of which the Amish would in actuality reject, having themselves been oppressed by such a theocracy in Europe).

But the Amish, too, have their opinions about the modern assertion that the goal of life is individual happiness, based on a right to be whatever we choose—to "follow your bliss." They believe that this is a very dangerous notion for both the individual and society.

The cult of self denies that we come with strings attached, that we have a built-in nature that can't be remade at will. Both the Anabaptists (to which the Amish belong) and the Society of Friends have emphasized the reality of our human nature. We come into this world created in God's image, but we also share in the consequences of humanity's fall from grace, in our natural propensity to sin.

The modern says: "I can make myself any persona I choose. I am infinitely moldable and adaptable, the master of my own fate."

The plain Christian replies: "While it's true you can remake your facade and your personality, the real you—your soul—is still the same, and still in need of God's grace to be transformed."

People today are ostensibly exposed to the transforming power of therapy: You arrive on earth perfect and good, then bad things happen to you, so now you are broken and in need of mending. But the Christian message is just the opposite: You arrived here with a potentially fatal flaw, but by turning to Christ and handing your life over to Him (literally "dying to self" by replacing your wants and desires with His, instead of cultivating and healing your own self), you will be brought back into God's kingdom.

In my Friends meeting last week, one of the ministers (not a plain, Wilburite type, but a humble Quaker soul) stood partway through an otherwise totally silent worship and began speaking:

There is no other way, my Friends; "Except you be regenerated and born again, ye cannot inherit the kingdom of God." This is the word of the Lord God to all people this day.

Anyone in meeting may be called to speak; those who are regularly called on by the Spirit are more formally recorded and spoken of as ministers. This minister is self-effacing, halting, and slow of speech in everyday conversation. But when he is standing before the congregation, his demeanor is that of one with authority, and the words are deliberate and well paced:

> There is no other way, Friends. This fact is not some airy whim or vain imagined half-truth, and whatever else you may be striving for, you must, *every particular man and woman,* be born again, else you cannot enter the Kingdom of Heaven. This was the doctrine of Christ, given even as He appeared in the world and preached it to Nicodemus. This is a standing doctrine to this very moment, and will be while any person yet breathes upon the earth; there is no other way, no other gate to enter into life, but by this great work of regeneration.

Mary Ann and I sit near the back so that the children on our laps won't disturb others (but Tasha and Jack have already come to appreciate and share in the quiet of our way of worship). We're leaning forward, listening intently to this challenging message—"There is no other way!" In today's world such statements are rightly feared, since they usually are issued by the power-hungry, by those with their own personal agenda they would impose as a stepping-stone to power over others. But to be called by the Prince of Peace to a transformed life in Him—we don't fear that calling but rather welcome it with open hearts and minds.

Today the modern libertine spirit is as powerful and hence as dangerous as the spirit of demogogy present in some right-wing religious groups. They're two sides of the same coin: The philosophy of complete freedom is growing monstrous in its pursuit of pleasure, and to restrain it, the "ayatollahs" are requesting that ever-stronger social controls be placed in their hands. With no cultural middle of civility and morality, America dangerously ricochets between decadence and tyranny.

For the Amish living in this little community through which I am slowly making my way on foot, a domain of self-imposed morality has stretched into every area of life. You can espy some of it in the orderliness of their homes and the rich, healthy diversity of the countryside. One of the larger barns off to one side of the road was undoubtedly built by group labor, and it is safe to assume that none of those who helped had insurance, nor did the owner. Though the danger of a lawsuit in case of injury exists in theory, the truth is that no Amishman would be permitted by conscience or community to take his loss to court. And he could in turn rightfully trust that the community itself will take care of its own. Fulfilling one's duty to another— raising his barn, and doing so from a perspective of trust rather than fear—is a small but significant proof that the Amish have left behind the larger society's domain of laws and freedoms. The power of either coercion or hedonism to blot out freely chosen virtue has been held in check here.

What does modern life offer between the positions of exploiter and victim, other than an imagined penaltyless freedom to follow one's bliss? Yet this fantasy bliss is often chosen to avoid conforming to a standard. We humans seem to prefer not to accept the pressing fact that actions always have consequences.

When we lived in Sugarcreek, Amish on all sides, Mary Ann sometimes felt self-conscious about hanging out the family laundry on days other than those specified by the Amish way (Monday for the main load, Wednesday for follow-up loads, maybe an extra line of diapers on Saturday). Going against the unanimous pattern, even though she wasn't obligated by communal ties, seriously intimidated her.

We came to give a shorthand description of the communal blueprint of our neighbors as the "Amish kit." In terms of household life, this kit is a compendium of tried-and-true ways to do things. Today on my walk I can see the evidence of it all around me. The house I am coming up to is almost identical with its neighbors in every important respect. It has two stories above a walk-out basement banked into the earth on its back side. The basement is ringed with windows—it's a sunny basement for people who don't light the way with electricity. It is also cool, and, with the walk-out door serving as a handy entrance for garden produce, it undoubtedly sports a canning kitchen. In the summer the family food preservationist can work all day here without getting overheated. The basement probably has few interior walls so that it can serve as a cool location for church services, which are held in homes on a rotating basis. The big open area can be strung with clothesline in the winter for cold-weather indoor clothes drying. It all makes sense, fits together, *works*.

The rationality of such parts of the Amish kit draws the occasional envy of the modern mind with its more fractured daily life. Other particulars are baffling. Far up a hill I can see a lone man and horse plowing a garden. Why do the Amish not allow tractors in the field? Why don't tractors fit into the kit? Some writers on the Amish describe this decision as a sort of tribal taboo. Is the man on the hill just a slave to an unexamined tradition?

In reality, the Amish long ago banished tractors from the farm for a good reason: Tractors would reduce the need for communal fieldwork and thus induce autonomy. People would need one another less and would be led away from servanthood. They would separate from each other. It was also foreseen that tractors would eliminate the horse from the farm, allow quicker trips to town, and eventually result in automobile ownership. From that perspective, I think the fellow on the hill toiling behind the horse and plow looks pretty smart, pretty cutting-edge in his critique.

While the average Amish adult may not be ready to explain church rules in exactly these terms, each person would certainly say that such use of the tractor is too "high," too worldly. (In Geauga County I have heard the Amish refer to the rest of the people there as *der Hicht*, "the high ones," although this is rare, because name-calling is also forbidden.) They would point to the larger society's rural situation, which has amply borne out their fears about the use of tractors.

I am walking through an Amish church district of nearly identical well-tended homesteads, sensibly laid out in the midst of healthy and fertile farmlands. There are children out-of-doors, all dressed more or less alike; they are safe and happy. Is this conformity a bad thing?

It certainly isn't mindless. This conforming to a higher good is quite intentional, a willed emptiness of self that God lovingly fills. See the fruits of it here? Blessed are they who abandon self-will, leaving room for God to fill up their lives with His order and righteousness. *Blessed are the poor in spirit: for theirs is the kingdom of heaven.*

It's warmer now, and although I took off my coat a few miles back, the sweatshirt also has to go in the pack. The road has begun to climb. I can hear for the first time the roar of cars on the freeway to the north. The road I am on turns in that direction, and after a while I can see the interstate ahead of me. My hurt knee has started to ache a lot more, especially when I walk downhill, as I am doing at the moment, dragging my right leg a little over the gravel as I try to keep the knee stiff.

As the road flattens out, the freeway visible about a mile ahead, I notice my feet are hurting, too, particularly the left one, which has had to compensate all day for my weakened right leg. I have to stop and sit down, take off the shoe, and massage my foot for a while before continuing. Finally the highway is just ahead, and I turn onto a country road that runs parallel to it. I'm really in some agony now. I have to stop and sit on the grass more frequently, resting there with my pack beside me until I can hoist myself back up by the staff.

At various times today I have muttered small prayers to God, asking for the strength to continue on this day's journey. Now I find myself asking more forcefully, Why me? Why do I have to have so much pain on the first day? Strangely enough (since I haven't really expected a reply), the answer comes so quickly and powerfully that it makes my tired and hurting body pause and sway around the axis of the staff: "Why you? Because you're fifteen pounds overweight and didn't think you needed to train very hard for the walk!"

Well, there's an answer for you. Pain is there to tell us something. It's telling me that I haven't learned the entire lesson of today's beatitude. Putting myself fully in God's hands without doing my own part—that is, training until I was really ready to take this hike—shows that I was in fact willing to commit myself to His leading only to a certain degree. Where was the single-mindedness that would have considered more closely what was required of me to go forward under His direction? It was my own weakness, my own double-mindedness, that allowed me to ignore the obviously necessary detail of being physically fit.

I have made it to the highway that zips east and west across Ohio's midsection. My country lane soon puts me alongside the back fence of a highway rest stop. There are more trucks parked here than cars, more trucks on the highway as well. Interstate 70 is probably the busiest east-west

route for hauling freight, just as was once true of its prede-
cessor, the National Road of many years ago, even before it
became Route 40.

The Teamsters didn't start as a truckers' union. Teamsters were men (and, very occasionally, women) who
hauled material in wagons pulled by teams of horses and
mules. A teamster of the early 1800s might haul as much
weight in his twenty-foot-long wagon as a modern semitrailer can hold. Multiple hitches of up to twelve horses
were not uncommon sights along the National Road in
its day.

The town I am hoping to reach this evening was once
an important stop for teamsters headed for western Ohio
or returning to Maryland on the National Road. It still fills
a similar role as the major truck stop between Wheeling
and Zanesville on Interstate 70. Old Washington, now that
I can see it coming into view across the interstate, looks
much the same as I would guess it did when the wagons
rolled through its main avenue in the 1830s.

The pain in my legs is harder to ignore. I feel as if I am
close enough now to rest as often as needed—about every
thousand feet or so. I can see the fairgrounds across the
highway, and just past them my road ends, leaving me to
turn right and cross over the interstate on a high bridge.
Making my way across at a near crawl, my body is shaken
by shock waves from trucks hurtling beneath me and the
unending rumble of cars traveling back and forth on the
bridge. People are returning home from work. It must be
after five o'clock.

I'm glad I don't have to commute across this bridge

with Ned. He's not the sort of horse to take all this shaking in stride.

Now on the other side of the highway below, I can walk just a short way downhill—maybe half a mile—to an underpass that leads *back* across the interstate and over to the truck stops along the exit ramps. The ancient village of Old Washington has its back to me and the interstate; the buildings line themselves up on both sides of the former National Road, now a state highway, Route 40. The road I am walking on is parallel to 40, just a back lane that ends at the underpass beneath the freeway.

Turning my back on Old Washington, I take the underpass road in hundred-foot increments, resting periodically on the guardrail as I go. The truck stop motel room (nine dollars for a small, clean room without a television) is entombed in a huge 1950s atomic-style blinking nightmare-in-the-round concrete edifice just ahead.

Once inside the glass doors, I see it is actually calmer and better designed than I would have guessed. It feels good to put my leg up in the motel's restaurant booth. I order something, though I don't feel hungry. At home my family will be eating supper about now. They will begin by giving thanks for the food; usually we ask the blessing silently, heads bowed. (Susanna is granted the toddler exemption, and is probably looking around at everyone.) I bow my head here in the restaurant. Although we shouldn't give a second thought as to whether it is proper to pray in public (it is), the content of our thanksgiving sometimes is so personal, between ourselves and God, that it would hardly be right to tell about it.

The beans and white rice are fine, but I don't eat much. I want to find my room. When I lie down in bed a few minutes later, my aches and pains tell me that I have indeed walked almost thirty miles today—a lot of it in the wrong direction, and with a serious knee injury. I feel so dizzy. This would be the hour to say good night to Jack and Susanna, and I say good night to them now, along with Tasha and her mother. The freeway somehow roars by just a few feet from where we are sitting together in the living room, and I see it outside the window, like some sort of mechanical ocean on which our little Barnesville home is sailing toward Columbus.

The Second Day

Blessed are they that mourn: for they shall be comforted.

Last night I hoped my body would repair itself a little bit before this morning. Today's section of the trip is not so long—only about fifteen miles—with no chance to get lost again, but I can tell as I swing my lower half off the bed that it is going to be rough. The right knee and left foot both send thick, liquid jolts of pain up my legs. I won't be able to put much weight at all on that knee. I look around for my staff and see that it stayed with me on the bed all night. Thank you, Lord, for Your buckeye tree. After dressing and buying a banana and muffin at the restaurant counter, I head out the door.

Across the street at Matt's Mountaintop Stop truck plaza a moving sign towers sixty feet above the freeway. It gives the time as 5:04 and the temperature as nineteen degrees. Out comes the ski mask from my pack.

Moving about as slowly as a person can without falling down, I cross back over into Old Washington and take a left turn—westward—at the main intersection. Now I am on State Route 40. Under my feet is the old National Road, and underneath *that* is the dirt path of Zane's Trace, the first white man's trail into eastern Ohio.

This section of Route 40 today is little more than a local circuit for commuters around Old Washington and the county seat in Cambridge, Ohio. Yet, if one wanted to, it could be driven or walked all the way to Indianapolis without any significant detours.

The road lies flatter than I expected. This area was supposedly shaped by glaciers into a series of long, steep grades and hills, but the newer road cuts through these for the most part. From the passenger seat of a car recently I noticed the narrowness of the berms along this stretch, but on the ground they don't seem too bad yet.

The steep banks of the hills through which the roadway plows are keeping the early morning sun away. The lower half of the front of my ski mask is coated with ice. A look over my shoulder, however, rewards me with a brilliant pink sky. Back home the sun would be nowhere near coming over the ridge up at the barn, but I would be up and shaking Tasha awake to help me with the feeding of the animals. I'd have some time for silent prayer while Tasha dresses, and then together we would bring water up the hill.

On a morning like this the worlds of the house and barn have little in common. The house on the hillside is still dark and sleepy, just beginning to warm. At the top of the hill, however, we are greeted with bright sunshine and the calls of goats and cats who sense our arrival even before the door to the barn is opened. Inside, the barn feels warm after the cold walk up the hill, and the animals are alert and anticipating some breakfast. The door in Ned's stall that leads to the pasture is opened to let in more streams of light as pails and troughs are filled with water and grain. These days of spring make Ned want to head right out to eat the newly sprouted grass that grows out of the snow in light green bunches. This new grass is rich fare after a winter of baled hay, and Ned's time outdoors has to be rationed while he gets used to it. More than an hour out in the pasture, and Ned could literally eat himself to death.

Tasha is a good worker, and I can count on her to pay attention to such details while I am here on the dark, cold road. Now I need to stop for a moment in the driveway of a trailer park to paw around inside my coat and retrieve the Sermon on the Mount—something to concentrate on despite my knee and the cold. My driver's license has worked itself into the tiny pamphlet and bookmarks the correct place:

Blessed are they that mourn: for they shall be comforted.

I repeat this second beatitude to myself over and over, turning its meaning through my mind. Barclay saw this saying of Jesus as picturing the man who is sorrowing with the knowledge of his own unworthiness, his own sin:

Christianity begins with a sense of sin. Blessed is the man who is intensely sorry for his sin, the man who is heartbroken for what his sin has done to God and to Jesus Christ, the man who sees the Cross and is appalled by the havoc wrought by sin.

Being sorry for turning from God—that's the first step *toward* God, isn't it? As soon as we repent, God is upon us, comforting and forgiving us. "The way to the joy of forgiveness is through the desperate sorrow of the broken heart," Barclay concludes.

Once, in a confrontational moment with a relative who has embraced a particular hodgepodge of Native American religion, Victorian spiritism, magic, and gnostic Christianity (it's all bundled together, but I have no idea what it's called), I tried to encourage her with the thought that we were all praying for her. As you might surmise, this was not received as it was intended, producing instead an angry yet telling reply: "Don't pray for me! My God loves me *just the way I am!*"

It's true that God loves us wherever we may now be in our relationship to Him, but I think it would be a terrible mistake to believe that He is content for us to *stay* where we are.

Taken together with yesterday's experience, this beatitude seems to follow from the previous one. When we give up on the idea that we can master life, we instantly see for the first time how thoroughly we have resisted God and His will for us. I think of this particularly when it comes to my own children. When Tasha was a three-year-old, she began to throw horrible fits. Whether it was how we had raised her up to that point or simply a combination of a phase she was going through and her own naturally strong will, these fits were difficult to control and seemingly impossible to eradicate. Discipline, punishment, reward, even just holding her in our arms for long periods—nothing seemed to help. As they continued, I found myself making things worse for her by becoming increasingly impatient, to the point where she could sense my dislike for her.

During this time I rarely asked God for help, and even then it was only to ask that *my* will be done. Mostly, I looked for answers that were within my power to implement and control, searching in parenting books for the secular trick that would bring Tasha back to herself. But I was under my own power, really just another self-willed child—and I contributed to her difficulty, because in this state I could not offer her the security she would have felt, troubled as she was, in the arms of a mature, loving parent.

How things have changed, though! Prayer has replaced the advice of parenting therapists, and we seem to be so much calmer, happier, and more secure as a family. (Most days!) For us, loving firmness has been the answer, modeled after our own relationship with the Lord.

At home it would be almost the time for morning devotion, so I sing today's song:

> Everywhere I go the Lord is near me
> When I call upon Him He will hear me
> Never will I fear
> For the Lord is near
> Everywhere I go.

The Zane-ette, a roadside relic of 1950s popular culture, sits on the left near the pavement, selling dairy and ice cream treats. Closed until summer. Its name is a paean to the road I am on, which began as an Indian trail, later known as Zane's Trace.

Now the gravel past the road's edge does in fact peter out, leaving nothing to walk on but the pavement or deep ditches on both sides of the road. I hop into one of these several times to avoid oncoming traffic. Hobbling in and out of the ditch is tiring to my knee, so I give up and just keep walking down in the ditch.

An incredibly steep brick road winds down from the clifflike ridge to my left. The road sign I pass has been attached to its post in an absurd, makeshift fashion, so that only the first two and last two letters of the street name are visible. Automatically I think of a word game to play with Tasha, although she isn't here with me. The letters are Br——se; what is the name of the road? Brick House? Breakaway Horse? That last might make sense on such a steep incline.

Tasha's emotional health has gradually caught up with her quick and flexible mind, so that together they yield humorous intensity. As she has been raised without television, her sense of verbal humor is never of the sassy, sophisticated sort. Her precocity remains innocent, for the most part:

> *Tasha:* What would be a bad government for
>   pioneers?
> *Me: (Perplexed silence—is this a real question or one
>   of her word jokes?)* I don't know.
> *Tasha:* A frontyranny!

Tasha: What do you call supermarket apples fixed
   up to be sold without their permission? *(She
   can hardly contain herself.)*

Tasha: Waxation without representation!

The road drops lower and lower and picks up Zane's
Trace from where it had wandered up a ridge and away
from Route 40 the last few miles. The berm reappears as
I descend onto a wide plain that leads to Leatherwood
Creek, near Cambridge. It's scrubby-looking land, clogged
with industrial plants and construction-supply warehouses.

Once it was the unveiling place of the Leatherwood God.

In the Leatherwood Valley of the 1820s, several of the
local denominations held revival meetings in a makeshift
pavilion. This was in the midst of the Second Great Awak-
ening of religious fervor along the American frontier. At
one of these revivals a short man clothed in buckskin
seemed to suddenly and magically appear at the pulpit, his
wild and fiery eyes flashing and his waist-length black
beard waving back and forth as he made strange, horselike
snorting noises. Although it seems thoroughly ridiculous
today, the crowd of that time was impressed—at least most
of them were. Without giving any other name, he declared
that he was God and that the end was about to be brought
down on them by his doing. The local pastors took him in
and publicly "worshiped" him in their churches, while he
preached the countdown to Armageddon. Then, of course,
he disappeared, taking with him a lot of love offerings and
church funds.

Everyone involved was embarrassed, especially when they later heard he'd spent all their money in Pittsburgh. The Quakers, of whom there were several hundred in the vicinity, are not known to have played any role in the fiasco. This is as one would expect, given their reclusiveness, their lack of interest in paid preaching and revival movements, and their own well-developed system of checks and balances on people's individual mystical experiences. If it contradicted Scripture, or even just the group sense of the Divine, an individual's revelation was regarded as probably a fancy or imagining. If any Friends had been present, they would have told the Leatherwood God he had "gone beyond his gift" and "gotten up into apostasy," as the Friends founder George Fox said of one early member who went off the deep end as a self-appointed messiah.

By the mental gauge I've been using to measure distance, which is to imagine I'm walking to Barnesville (that radio tower up ahead is as far as the end of my street; the next mailbox is as far as the meetinghouse), I've come about six miles—to Barnesville and back and then partway there again. Once the road starts back uphill, I have to stop every half mile or so. A routine develops of sitting on a guardrail post, dropping the pack, propping the staff, taking off my left shoe, and squeezing and massaging my foot for several minutes. About two miles up the hill I round a bend and see the I-70 exchange at Cambridge. It is much closer than I thought. One more rest stop and I am crossing the bridge over the highway, then sitting down in a fast-food restaurant with a cup of coffee (Quaker beer, my friend Seth calls it, disapproving of any and all vice). With my shoes off, my sore feet can rest, discreetly propped up under the table by the seat across from mine.

Outside the window cars stop and start in a line at the drive-through, bored, almost mechanical looks on the faces behind the windshields. The cashier who sold me the coffee wore the same expression as she rang up my purchase while listening to the headset earphone connecting her to the line of cars.

It certainly isn't her fault, this bored disconnection from reality. It's a widespread condition. Rubbing my swollen foot under the table, I recall that the two people who sold me these shoes seemed equally distant. I usually try to be extra ingratiating in such situations, feeling a bit as though it must be me, personally, that they find so uninteresting. But it is, as I said, a societal affliction.

This morning I haven't made any attempt to brighten someone's day—the cashier's, for instance. On the trip so far I've been much more reserved and less talkative than usual. So I'm keeping my distance, too. At least for now.

I think it's because this trip is a solitary journey. I need to witness, to simply observe and think and feel, and not really participate in the day-to-day life going on around me.

Only half of today's walk is finished. I'm wondering how to continue with this level of discomfort. After half an hour of staring out the window, I put on my shoes and continue on my way. It's uphill again for a mile into Cambridge proper.

Route 40 through Cambridge is called Wheeling

Avenue. Coming onto the town square, one can see almost exactly the view that appears in George R. Stewart's history of the National Road, *U.S. 40: Cross Section of the United States of America*. Stewart followed 40 all the way from Atlantic City, New Jersey, to the place where it ends, at Tenth Street in San Francisco, California. He took pictures along the way as the basis for his book, and in so doing left a marvelous record of the places along the Road as they appeared in 1949–50.

Most of the buildings in his shot of Cambridge were already old in Stewart's time, but they are all still standing. The large elm tree on the square seems to be gone, however, probably a victim of the Dutch elm disease that made short work of most urban canopies. In his text Stewart singled out the tree for mention:

> The gigantic elm tree shadowing the square suggests an age well over a century, and is recorded as having been a large tree as early as 1840. It must therefore antedate the arrival of the National Road at Cambridge in 1826; in all probability it was already well established in 1806 when the town was founded. Possibly the street was actually laid out to pass this tree.

I duck into a downtown restaurant for lunch, one not visible in Stewart's photo but plainly one of the older buildings in town. Many of the downtown buildings, including those on either side of me, are, like the ones in

Barnesville, holdovers from the national building spree of the 1880s, which left rural towns such as this with an over-abundance of space. Today, most of the serious retailing is happening at one of the two freeway interchanges outside Cambridge, where the box stores, the McDonald's and Bob Evans restaurants, and the larger supermarkets peddle their global wares. Here in the village's center are some banks, restaurants, and antiques and thrift shops—as well as the law offices—that are found in the vicinity of every county's courthouse.

To fathom why there would be anything here at all—to understand why this is a *place*—it is necessary to go back in time even further than the advent of the National Road, on back to the path through the "wilderness" taken by Ebenezer Zane.

Trail blazing back in the late 1700s was a form of entrepreneurship at least as much as it was a result of pioneer spirit. If you could cut a road to your own land claim, then the people who came after you would be buying from your store, paying for you to ferry them across the river, settling in the town you had already laid out. Zane was just such an experienced storekeeper in the backwoods, and an Indian-fighting frontiersman, when he made his entrepreneurial deal with the U.S. government in 1796 to cut a road into the "Ohio country" from the settled village of Wheeling, now in West Virginia.

In exchange for making the road, he would be granted three mile-wide tracts of land. The first of these was on the banks of the Muskingum River (where he also established the first of his moneymaking ferries). The part of his road, Zane's Trace, leading to the city he laid out on his mile-square tract became the eastern Ohio leg of the National Road. The town, of course, became the present-day city of Zanesville.

I can appreciate Zane's courage and grasp his eco-nomic motives, but his lead of the westward expansion, powered as it was by the hatchet and the gun, is only one side of the European experience in America. It is partly my heritage, too. One of my ancestors was among the Scots-Irish warrior clans that pushed across Pennsylvania, Ohio, and Virginia with pistols blazing, killing and driving the American tribes before them. But Zane's Trace also leads to the present, in which the land I found on the old coal road is being killed and driven before the bulldozers. As poet and farmer Wendell Berry said twenty years ago, "One cannot help but see the similarity between this for-eign colonialism and the domestic colonialism that, by policy, converts productive farm, forest, and grazing lands into strip mines."

The National Road in all its incarnations is a central technology of expansionism and exploitation. One gets the sensation while walking along its undeviating westward path that it lays open the land on either side—cuts through it and thus eviscerates it. Stewart subtitled his book on U.S. 40 *Cross Section of America,* which can mean in part that the road is an opening, an incision into which white settlers reached to pull forth something of value.

It is also a road with many layers in the vertical, a time machine showing all at once the periods of striving and collapse during our blind expansion. The concrete super-highway that runs alongside it and the rail beds that do likewise are also artifacts of the road. Under its pavement are the bricks that by government decree were laid down to facilitate the movement of troops and war materiel during the First World War. And beneath that is the sketchy, dirt-packed trace, with stumps cut just below the height of a wagon's running gear. According to Stewart, the Road followed the fleeing native inhabitants:

In the summer of 1796 Zane began work on the road with a party of six or eight men. They blazed trees, cleared out the thick underbrush, and re-moved fallen tree-trunks. They had pack-horses with a tent and provisions, but they lived largely on game. Two men kept watch at night, for there was still some fear of Indians, in spite of their defeat at the Fallen Timbers in 1794.

The trail-makers followed the course of the Wheeling Creek for about seven miles. After that they took the road up to the ridge, and kept on westward, generally avoiding marshy lands and keeping high, after the manner of Indian trails. In some places they may actually have followed the old Mingo Trail.

So here I am in their footsteps, although I am coming west not to seek my fortune but to give something away. Besides the warrior clans, I have more peaceful relations in my family tree. As I said, the introduction of Europeans to the Americas wasn't solely modeled after Cortés and John Smith of Jamestown. The Quakers (several of whom show up in the elaborate family genealogies produced by my late aunt Norma) settled among and lived peacefully with the native people throughout the early part of William Penn's "Holy Experiment" in settling the colony of Pennsylvania.

They purchased land at fair prices and honored their treaties. More important from the Native American point of view, the Friends believed in and practiced loving kindness toward all persons, and expected the same in return. This was a novel turn of events for a native culture that had come to expect lies and death from Europeans. In the 1600s and early 1700s the Friends were repaid for their respectful behavior with lasting peace. The net result was that they lived in greater security and prosperity than many settlers in less enlightened colonies.

The "Quaker peace" ended when the rich and arrogant sons of Penn took land that belonged to the native inhabitants, and land-hungry Scots-Irish immigrants began pouring into western Pennsylvania, cheating and provoking the Indians. Penn's boys didn't even pretend to profess Friends' beliefs on the subject, and the immigrants in particular "did not share the Quaker view of the Indian," wrote historian Margaret Bacon in her study of American Friends, *The Quiet Rebels*. Thus the Scots-Irish frontiersmen "were quick to respond to the slightest sign of Indian truculence or discontent."

This Road that speeds by outside the restaurant where I sit in solitude over a too-hot bowl of soup is a double-minded road, with two definite and separate uses. One—

the more prevalent—is as a means to exercise power over others, the strong over the weak. That is the coal road, the mercantile road, the invading path of Zane's Trace. But at the same time the Road fulfills another agenda. It is an agency for peaceful settlement, an invitation to peacefully become part of a place. Before the Quakers ever used the Road to enter Ohio, they sent tools and seeds on it to their friends the Delaware, whose tribes had settled along the Muskingum after being pushed out of the East. When the Friends did cross the river into Ohio, it was from North Carolina and Virginia, where they could no longer abide the institution of slavery.

Whole entire meetings picked up and moved themselves to the eastern part of Ohio in the years 1800–18. They settled peacably and grew into well-ordered, fruitful communities. To find an instructive example today of how they developed a graceful way of living in place, you would need to walk through the Amish district I found along the road yesterday—or any of the hundreds like it. To understand how either of these alternatives to the "violent route" came about, I think you would have to consider today's beatitude:

Blessed are they that mourn: for they shall be comforted.

Inside the pacifism of the plain people (or nonresistance, as many prefer), there is something of "the man who sees the Cross and is appalled by the havoc wrought by sin." Even as we rejoice that Jesus let Himself be made a final offering and atonement for our sins, we can also apprehend our own complicity in making the sacrifice necessary, and our own hand in accomplishing the violence done to the Son of God.

With our eyes so fixed on the Cross, we can be led to

a penitent life. Perhaps my journey to Columbus comes partly out of that impulse to ask for and be granted forgiveness. Absentmindedly musing about the trip causes me to fish around in my pocket and hand the waitress my driver's license instead of money. After a moment's confusion I pay my bill and start to leave. Bright light floods in through the door ahead. It's a beautiful day. Soon I am limping across a bridge over the old rail yard and beginning the climb up a steep and winding hillside that would give Ned, my horse, a workout.

I think I must look a sight. I am, after all, practically standing still, or even seeming to move backward now and then, as I try to will my injured limbs to work for me. Oh, this is bad! The world weaves back and forth under the edge of my hat brim in a sickening dance as I inch along a concrete drainage ditch. The ditch, filled with muck and leaves, provides the only footing next to this busy section of the road.

A woman in a white luxury car slows and opens her window: Would I like a ride?

Boy, would I. At the outset of the trip, however, I made a plan that each time I was offered a ride I would say, "No, thanks. Can you tell me what time it is?" the idea being that having a ready-made response would help me resist the tempting offer of a ride, yet by asking the time I would still give the offerer a way to be of help.

"No, thank you; can you tell me the time?"

Her answer is blown away by the air brakes of a descending truck: "Five past—" something. I nod and shout my thanks so she can lead away the growing line of cars behind her. Watching the lot of them roaring and smoking up the hill, I think how violent cars are when you experience them from the outside. Inside, all is comfy and smoothly serene, just like in the television commercials, but out here there's a lot of noise and the feeling that the world is being slammed to pieces by all those tires.

> *Blessed are the poor in spirit: for theirs is the kingdom*
> *of God.*
> *Blessed are they that mourn: for they shall be comforted.*

Reciting the first two beatitudes together now, toiling up the hill, good old foot and knee in the worst pain yet experienced . . . It occurs to me that I'm never going to finish this trip. I'll sink if I continue under my own power! So I ask God for help—really ask with all my might: God, I'm sorry! I've been trying to do this without your help, and I know I can't. Please, please help me!

And immediately the pain goes away.

Well, I mean, *come on!* A particle of modern suspicion and skepticism still hides out somewhere in my mind, and it doesn't react kindly to this event. Too much like Jimmy Swaggart or something. In fact, I remember back before I believed in God—back in the librarian days—I used to bring books to an elderly shut-in named Lola, and all Lola seemed to do was read her Bible and watch television evangelists. Her TV had a negative spiritual effect on me.

Lola's favorite video preacher was a jowly, smirking fellow who, to my horror, sounded like he was snickering in mocking glee as he ordered the old ladies in TV land to send their money so he could heal them. Then the program would cut to a taped revival meeting where he would be calling up sick people and waving his jewel-encrusted fingers at them. Then big, tough-looking altar guys would rush up behind the sick folk and "catch" them as they "fainted"—by knocking their legs out from under them. It was pretty bad, but it really impressed Lola.

"Buddy, I tell you"—Lola always called me, and everybody else, Buddy—"that man can *heal*. He's got hisself God's own Holy Spirit a-workin' in them hands."

But it also comes back to me how humbly grateful Lola was for every little thing in life. Just waking up and putting on her glasses after a nap caused her to praise the Lord. The TV faith healer never healed her—I doubt she ever even thought of asking him to—yet her faith in the healing power and love of her Maker was absolute.

I came to Lola with a secret childhood grudge against the reward-centered religion of my parents. What I understood of their belief was that God blesses materially those who seek His favor.

Right now, the same irritation I felt against that Divine quid pro quo when I was a child comes back to me: *In the midst of so much suffering in the world, why would it be fair for God to correct my little leg problem?*

Jesus' answer is "Your faith has made you well." Lola's answer was her life, which I didn't understand at the time, a life that didn't seek an earthly reward in return for loving God. Forget about that, Buddy. Trust in God, ask Him for what you need, praise Him regardless of how—to your tiny, limited discernment—He appears to respond. Have faith in Him single-mindedly, love Him single-heartedly, because the real reward is to be completely with Him in eternity. And you might run into Lola up there, too.

Now all of me is saying *Thanks be, praise be to God.* I'm still stiff and have to move slowly cresting the hill, but there isn't any pain in either my knee or my foot. I look around me at the trees and meadows with a heightened consciousness. The world is aglow.

Maybe I'm just going crazy, and my real destination is to be a wild-eyed street preacher in Columbus. But I'm singing aloud anyway:

Everywhere I go the Lord is near me!
When I call upon Him, He will hear me!

Until now, walking downhill has been particularly painful to my knee, but I am realizing that I have learned a new gait that takes away the pain. In fact, it feels good, as though my knee is getting a helpful treatment by holding my leg a certain way as I swing it forward. Frankenstein's monster on a pilgrimage. I must look ridiculous.

Reciting the beatitude again, I stop for a rest at the S-shaped bridge outside of New Concord, my destination for today. The bridge is off to the side of the main road, which curves past it. Its single arch of stone spans a creek. The curves at the top and bottom of the S follow the retaining walls that hug the banks for a short while prior to and after the crossing. Stewart, in his book on the National Road, unearthed an engineer's explanation for oddly shaped bridges such as this one along the Road:

> The stone arches of the bridges are all so constructed as to cross the stream at a right angle to its course. . . . A bridge thus built is the shortest one possible, and so uses the least material. . . . Since the fastest moving traffic was hardly at more than 10 miles an hour, there was no safety-factor involved, and the traveler was scarcely inconvenienced.

The bridge provides a pretty and shady spot to rest before coming into New Concord. Its tidy stone masonry seems to fit the definition of "good work" that I aspire to as a homesteader, and as a printer and editor of the magazine I help publish.

Moving again up the last big hill into New Concord, I get to enjoy the luxury of a smooth and level sidewalk set a few feet away from the road. I also notice there is a sizable blister on my big toe.

Tonight is my only expensive stay along the route, at a private inn that's several cuts above what I need in the way of lodging. Janet, the proprietress, is fascinated with me and wants to hear the details of my trip. But really, it's too much. I need a bath, a chance to soak my blisters and lie down for a while. I'm scheduled to speak tonight to a group of students at the local college here; Janet looks a little as though she doesn't believe me when I tell her this by way of explaining that I need to rest. I don't really look like a lecturer, I guess. Oh, I want that bath!

Finally we work out all I need to know about getting in and out of the place, and I'm shown to my room. The first thing I do is take the coverlet off the bed and drape it in a ceremonial fashion over the sleek little black television. I don't want to look at it, and I don't want its blank eye looking at me, either. There's no sense in leaving an opening to be tempted to waste any time in cable land. I dump the contents of my pockets on top of the coverlet: some change, the tract of beatitudes, and a section of map encased in plastic. My driver's license slips off and falls to the carpet, where I leave it for now.

After a long bath and a quiet time spent reading some books about New Concord's history that Janet thoughtfully left out for me, I drift off.

Having obtained a late supper some hours later in the student cafeteria, I walk up the steep campus hills and have a pleasant talk with the journalism students and their instructors. Now it is eight-thirty and I'm back already. At home this is the beginning of a tranquil hour or so, after the last child has been sent off to bed (departure times are by age in ascending order: seven, seven-thirty, eight). Mary Ann and I still sit across from each other at the dining room table, just like in the old days. Now, instead of searching frantically for answers, we read for relaxation or uplift, or we read and write letters.

Tonight I call her and we speak for a few minutes. It's a private conversation.

I feel the Road finally slipping away from me as I hang up the phone, and the night bringing on my rest.

The Third Day

Blessed are the meek: for they shall inherit the earth.

The day has started out cold again. But it warms up quickly, and I exchange mask for hat and remove the sweatshirt from under my coat. In my bleary-eyed preparations for leaving the inn this morning, I noticed my driver's license on the floor and scooped it up and into my coat pocket, where I can feel it now.

Stone mileposts erected in the days of the National Road have become more frequent today. Most of them have been painted white, with the incised names of towns and distances filled in with black. They are squat, about two and a half feet in height, and rounded at the top where the word *Cumberland* (Maryland, point of origin for the second leg of the road) and the number of miles to it appear. Beneath that, the stone's roundness is broken into two planes, one angled to the east and the other to the west, with the distance to Wheeling chiseled into the former and to Zanesville on the latter.

I walked along many roadsides as a teenager, but I

wasn't observing the negative effects of cars. Thumb out, ingratiating grin on my stubbly face, I was just trying to get into one of them. I hitchhiked everywhere I needed to go. For a while I lived in a sort of commune—it was the home of the single mother of one of my friends, but other than paying the bills, she didn't seem to have any control there. People would come and go and stay for weeks or months, keeping my friend's mom busy restocking the refrigerator and washing the linen. It was, really, a commune of *users:* users of the mom, users of drugs, sex, and alcohol, users of one another.

I wasn't the leader of it all, but I loved it. I thought it was great. So this was what it was like to finally have my own "family of choice" instead of my broken-down, unhappy "family of origin." In our makeshift commune we were all *so* happy . . . at least we were happy late into the night. In the morning we weren't so happy.

I remember one morning in particular. I had just woken up on a couch that someone had pushed onto the front lawn the previous evening, and I went upstairs to shower and shave. There were sleeping bodies here and there in the house, but nobody else was awake, even though a jazz album—Eric Dolphy's screeching saxophone train wreck, *Out to Lunch*—was blasting away at hundreds of decibels on auto replay in the living room.

Before she had left for a week's visit with relatives, the mom had hired a pest-control company to spray for fleas (we were a flea-bitten commune, to be sure). That particular morning a young woman in the pest company's uniform had driven up into the weeds and, getting no reply at the wide-open door, came on in and began to spray wherever there wasn't someone passed out. Eventually she made it to the bathroom, where I had just stepped from the shower and decided to shave before dressing. As the door swung open I turned into the concussive wave of atonal saxophone madness, and there she stood, her wide-mouthed scream swallowed up in *Out to Lunch*.

Running, screaming, hopping over bodies, she made for the pest truck and drove off in erratic bursts of speed.

I don't know that it is good for me to tell such stories. They bring back a perverse sort of pride I once had in how wild I could be. Did I win the prize? In truth, I wasn't as bad as I wished to appear, even at the commune. I was the only one who paid any rent, which meant I had to have an actual job. The commune was out in the country, about an hour's drive from the city where I worked as a record album salesman, and a good four miles from the nearest bus stop.

Every morning I would hitchhike my way to the bus stop, getting rides from basically the same few commuters who happened to be on the road during those hours. Being a record salesman was considered an unbelievably cool job among my set during that period of the 1970s, and I always dressed the part, in skinny tie, big wino hand-me-down suit jackets, black stovepipe jeans: the urban hippie look of 1976, recycled from the Beats of the 1950s and doomed to be recycled on into the future until the end of time or the end of MTV, whichever comes first. It's a wonder that basically normal people ever picked me up when my thumb was waving beside the road.

When I returned "home" at the end of each day, no one would give me a ride. I always had to walk the four miles back from the bus stop, and eventually I gave up on even signaling to the uncaring throng of late-day commuters whizzing by. These evening walks were good for me; they added some measure of health, fresh air, and exercise to the otherwise dissipated life I was pursuing. They made me the walker that I am now.

My short-term destination today is the National Road/Zane Grey Museum, four or five miles ahead and about ten miles before Zanesville. The road is straight and flat much of the way, and before I know it I'm standing outside the parking lot next to the museum. As I suspected, the museum is closed until the summer, and even then this is too early in the day to be let in. The museum itself looks rather dreadful from the outside, a lesser example of 1970s poured-concrete architecture that entombs space in ugliness.

Along this section of the Road there are numerous commercial buildings in various states of collapse, just as earlier on in the more rural sections of the journey there were broken and abandoned barns and farms. The structures I am passing look to have been thrown up hastily in an effort to skim off some of the dollars that once swam by along the Road. There is something inherently brash and temporary about them. The collapsed barns I have seen along the way trigger a deeper sense of loss, because I know they were built in the hope and expectation that they might be used and maintained for ages.

I dropped in on a barn raising once in Lancaster

County, Pennsylvania, just as the younger men were swarming along the top of the structure, nailing on the rafters for the roof. You could see inside the whole barn and observe how the massive wooden beams had been delicately joined together with green wooden pegs at the junctures of mortise and tenon. It was clearly visible that all the forces together—weight of the beams, hold of the pegs, connecting push of the rafters—cooperated to bring the barn into totality, into wholeness with itself. The humble parts were strong together. Take away any one and the structure would begin to lose its balance.

These commercial buildings are much simpler and coarser in their making and in their orientation. They are stick frames banged together like a lobster trap, set here to catch something.

That commerce has risen and fallen with the tide of the Road's fortune goes without saying. The growing traffic on the Road in the early 1800s was abruptly cut back by the advent of the canal system, and later the railroads. Taverns, liveries, and inns along this route opened and closed in response to the ebb and flow of travelers and teamsters. But time and again over the last two centuries, the National Road was rediscovered and brought back into wide use as a means to travel. In its most recent revival it was saved by the automobile, now traveling in the opposite direction of most previous Road movement—toward the east as men and materiel were trucked to the Atlantic Ocean and sent onward to Europe during World War I.

But the auto has also delivered what is probably the killing blow to this little two-lane history of America. Be-

fore cars, the pace of life along the Road made it more possible to weather the ups and downs. But once we began to
drive it, our demand for speed grew ever stronger, too
strong and fast for a mere two-lane road to handle, however mightily and swiftly the businesses along the edge
tried to keep up. When the traffic was abruptly diverted
onto the interstate highways, the hopped-up, strung-out,
grasping economy on the National Road took a tremendous fall. Here it lies, smashed alongside the pavement like
a twenty-car pileup of motels and eateries and car lots and
tourist shops.

See how completely and rapidly time has changed all,
and be humbled! Think of the men and their labor that
went into the paving of this street: thousands of miles of it
surfaced and resurfaced in the 1930s and 1940s, asphalt on
top of the carefully laid bricks—millions and millions of
bricks—that had been put down for the doughboys to roll
east on. All of this time and labor was superseded and dis-
carded a mere decade after the second big war, with the advent of the interstate.

I want to be an optimist. I wonder if it won't once again
spring to life, teeming with people looking for a slower way
to move through space than that offered on the freeway.
Maybe this time they'll come on bicycles or solar-powered
carts, or—who knows?—even in horse-drawn vehicles.

It isn't clear to me why the media mouthpieces of our
society are so absolutely certain that such a retrograde motion is impossible. Why do the futurists, the electronic
soothsayers and seers, so firmly believe that we will all live
in *Star Trek* reruns in the twenty-first century? They act as

if it is their duty to choose the future for us, and so they have begun to construct wide verbal ramps to funnel us onto their "information superhighway," all the while telling us it's what we want.

But we don't have to go along.

Certainly our children don't have to be a part of it. Despite all the dire warnings that children who are not strapped to the machine in infancy will be "left behind," we can choose to let them be just children. Tasha and Jack are learning—in the absence of talking machines—to talk with real, live people. They don't know Mr. Spock—they know Grandpa John. They have none of the media-created sense of forward motion, progress, technological destiny. Instead they experience their selves as living links in a generational chain that goes on without significant change, just as it has existed for centuries. We are constantly teaching them the past, so that they will carry their own link with them as they *become* the future. They aren't going to just *inhabit* someone else's technoid version of it.

I think it would really pay to stop listening to the futurists. What do Bill Gates and the other computer moguls really know about the road ahead? Maybe only about as much as Shelley's forgotten king:

And on the pedestal these words appear:
"My name is Ozymandias, king of kings:
"Look on my works, ye Mighty, and despair!"
Nothing beside remains. Round the decay
Of that colossal wreck, boundless and bare,
The lone and level sands stretch far away.

Across from the National Road/Zane Grey Museum is another futurist projection from the more recent past. An apparently still functioning motel from the 1950s struts its atomic-age stuff. The sign out front is a three-dimensional model of an atom made of large, cartoon-colored translucent balls on sticks of various lengths. I assume it is internally lit at night. Why does this place still look this way? Historic preservation? The obvious effort that has gone into maintaining it in its original form just as easily could have been directed toward remodeling it into a newer vernacular. Maybe this is the motelier's way of keeping the dream of the 1950s alive—the dream of zipping around in private spaceships, eating pills for food, talking to each other through tiny communicators.

In any case, this isn't the place to keep that dream going. The Jetsons will never stay at this out-of-the-way motel or swim in its "Olympic-size" pool. Much of the future is no longer a dream, anyway. Large parts have come true. Utopia as defined by the merchant class of the 1950s has arrived in the form of breakfast bars and cell phones. It's just that, well, now that it's here, some of us notice it's not so good. And refuse it.

Jack and Tasha don't see themselves as living in the past, but they do weigh their technological choices already. During one long and frustrating buggy trip with Ned, Mary Ann was grumbling about horse travel; this ride was an awful imposition on the children. I looked back at them: hot, tired, at least as out of sorts as their mother.

"Children, let's vote: nice new Toyota, or this impossible horse?"

Ned won, hands down.

I can see bits of the older brick paving underneath the thin and broken asphalt here as I start walking again toward the Interstate 70 exchange that lies just ahead. I head into the gas station to buy a cup of coffee and borrow the rest room key, just as the attendant is loudly boasting to the workmen hanging around the coffee urn that none of them could last the night with her. I try not to see the hardness in her face nor to hear the snorting guffaws of her admirers. She's someone I used to know, in a way. She might even be me as I used to be: full of guilt and without shame.

On the way to the rest room I pray for her, for me, for the workmen. Inside the rest room I take time to pray for the safety of my family while I'm away, and for my protection on the journey.

Drinking my cup of coffee on the embankment behind the gas station, I am again thinking of how my life and the lives of Mary Ann and the children have come to be progressively more sheltered from the rankness that seems to have overtaken American life.

First and foremost, we don't let television into our brains. Of course, everyone we know who has a television tells us that the only things watched on it are the "good shows," most often on public television or educational cable channels. We don't believe it. We like these folks, and don't think we would do any better than they at keeping the coarseness and stupidity of television out of the children's sight, so we don't even try, or—worse yet—fool ourselves. We just ban it.

We feel no guilt at not treating our children as little adults entitled to their own luxuries and vices. We are training them to cultivate character, so life is rather strict and the work is hard. But since we aren't offering them things as the expression of our love, they are getting a good bit of real, right-in-your-face love from us, mixed in with the firmness and all the chores.

When it comes to spending money, whom they play with, what they play at, and what is allowed versus what is not, our say is final. Do we listen to them, *ever?* Yes, of course, we weigh their desires and concerns constantly, because we love them and want them to be happy. But temporary happiness of the kind encouraged by pop culture is kept out of their grasp. While we are in the process of passing on the wisdom and worldview that have brought Mary Ann and me back to life, we will shield the children from much of the liberty other children experience.

Some of our relatives insist that by keeping television out of our home and refusing our children the adult freedoms now bestowed on many a preschooler, we are endangering them. We are overprotective; they should be basking in the larger society so that they are ready to defend themselves from it. After all, we can't protect them *forever!*

But since we can protect them *now,* while they are young, shouldn't we? The simplest mother rabbit hides her babies from the fox. Protecting the children while their character is forming is, of course, our first priority, just as it once was and should still be for all parents. Mary Ann responds to the issue with a question of her own: "If you

knew that a famine was approaching, how would you prepare your children? By starving them? Or by providing
them with lots of nutritious food?"

Or she tells this story: "When the government trains
experts to detect counterfeit money, it doesn't start out by
showing them lots of counterfeit money so they'll know
what it looks like. Instead, their training begins with them
examining real money—they look at real money closely,
over and over again, until they *really* know what it looks
like. Only then are they shown counterfeit money; their ex-
pertise in knowing real money makes it possible for them
to instantly spot the counterfeit."

Back on the road and skipping past the highway on
and off ramps, I feel as though I am traveling more quickly
and lightly today, as if my pack has been emptied of a burden. Maybe I'm starting to let God handle the journey. I
quickly settle into an easy pace, resting every few miles to
lengthen my endurance. Deep breaths, sunshine. The coat
and sweater both come off, and for the first time the spring
warmth allows me to walk in my shirtsleeves.

Soon the road is running parallel to the interstate,
which is only a few hundred yards away. Construction bar-
rels in the westbound lanes are slowing traffic. I would
guess it is about ten o'clock. It may be that Tasha and Jack
are passing by me on that very road right now. Some
friends of ours who drive are taking them to see a children's play in Columbus today, a special showing just for
home-schoolers from around the state.

I watch the traffic, hoping to spot their car. The play
they are on their way to is called *Linnea in Monet's Garden,*

after the book of the same title. Perhaps from my earlier description it sounds as if we keep the children behind barbed wire, but actually their experiences are varied, interesting, and . . . protected. Always the same question: Are we helping them to become good people? We know the world they'll be facing, and we want to prepare them to meet it with love, firmness, and sympathy, and as moral agents. (I freely recognize that every parent operating under this dictum will make different choices than we have; the Amish would never, ever let their children go to a city to attend a play. They consider cities and plays both more or less inherently corrupting.)

Trying to catch sight of Tasha and her brother makes me intensely lonesome for my children and for my wife. How glad it would make me to see two happy little figures waving to me from a car over there. I also worry for them a little bit, riding on the freeway. It seems more dangerous when you no longer often travel at such a high rate of speed.

They will have ridden the two hundred miles to Columbus and back, along with the time spent at the play, before I reach Zanesville today. It is much too far for my horse to go, so the car trip is a compromise to my plain way of living—or is it? It involves others sharing with us and our children, an activity at the trip's destination that we consider wholesome and good, the opportunity for our children to practice their manners . . . pretty plain, I'd say.

It also helps that we know they love horse travel much more than riding in a car. It is always assumed that children will be drawn to the flashy and fast things in life (popular culture is only too happy to surround them with such stuff). But our children, at least, seem to treasure a slower and less spectacular measure of travel, namely, Ned.

I brought my horse home in Fourth Month of 1996. We formed a parade up Cherry Ridge Road, two children and an infant in a stroller pushed by Mary Ann following him, me out in front leading the horse across the state highway and down the hill to his new home in our barn. I named him Ned.

I had to learn almost everything from scratch. Although I rode horses as a boy, my experience was akin to that of Little Lord Fauntleroy—somebody popped me into the saddle and later took me out, so I never saw where the horse came from, or where he went back to, let alone anything of his actual care and feeding. I took interest and pleasure in learning these things for the sake of Ned. I stacked hay in the loft and oats in the grain bin; learned to wash, comb, and brush him; picked out his hooves; kept fresh and full his five-gallon bucket of water.

An Amish draft horse trainer had already shown me how to put the bridle and harness on a plow horse, so it didn't take long to figure out the right methodology for connecting the driving harness to Ned and Ned to the buggy. I practiced driving Ned (that's all he really is, a horse to be driven, rather than a horse to be ridden or used for heavy fieldwork) for almost four months. I began by traveling every few days to Walnut Creek, a distance of two and a half miles, sometimes venturing a mile farther to the buggy shop that sits along the main road to Berlin. And then sometimes on to Berlin itself, a seven-mile trip each way, to visit the health food and feed stores. Toward the end of this time I was glad I had practiced the Berlin route, as it became necessary to get Jack to the doctor there one day.

To the automobile driver, these distances seem short, even to the point of being ridiculous. Imagine being so limited in mobility that a seven-mile trip seems like an accomplishment! However, it would probably make more sense to compare buggy travel with walking (which it more closely resembles) than with riding in a car. I suppose I could also draw a comparison between bicycles and buggies; they cover ground at similar speeds. But the experience of moving from place to place in a buggy is much closer to walking.

After I turned the final car in for recycling, I traveled all the winter and early spring on foot, sometimes pulling the children's red wooden "Berlin Flyer" wagon behind me to lug groceries from the Walnut Creek general store. Usually, though, I made unencumbered trips every few days on business to the print shop, the bank, or the post office. I got to know my neighborhood in a way that not even a bicycle would allow. I knew the songbirds and the ditches, the bridges and the particular silhouettes of the distant hills, quietly, intimately, as only the walkers of the world experience. Walking always leaves me feeling I have exited time to participate in the eternal "now" of creation. It puts me in a relationship of reverie and praise for all I see.

The most important route for our family, as we began to figure out where we needed to go in our newly carless life, was to the little village of Sugarcreek, about three miles away from home on the main road, going in the opposite direction from Walnut Creek. Sugarcreek has the IGA market, the blacksmith shop, and the hardware and feed stores, where we can trade money for whatever we haven't been able to either make ourselves or do without.

Mary Ann began sending me on fortnightly trips to Sugarcreek for groceries. Usually a few other tasks were thrown in, such as dropping off books at the one-room library or standing in line at the bank.

With thousands of Amish families and their buggies in the vicinity, Sugarcreek is a hospitable place to drive. If, however, you are the only buggy-driving Quaker in town, you have to be willing to endure stares not only from the tourists who throng Sugarcreek, but also from the Amish who don't know you.

At first I always took the back way into town, driving Ned along the winding dirt roads that allow horse-drawn vehicles to stay off the state highway cutting through the middle of this largely carless community. Ned was a skittish four-year-old when I bought him, and I was a skittish, inexperienced driver. I hoped that if I kept his flinching, rearing body off the main road, we would both have a safer journey. Not so. Every twist and turn of the road along the Cherry Ridge route to Sugarcreek brought a new—and for Ned, usually terrifying—vista. Ned has so far conveyed through remarkable and often unexpected gymnastics in the traces his fear of fence posts, round hay bales, road signs of every shape and size, hanging laundry, pigs, sheep, cows, and especially goats.

Ned's greatest fear is of Nelson Hershberger's "Goat in the Road." I don't know her name, or why Nelson lets her spend her summer days asleep on a long tether in the middle of our road. During the hottest weather, when my horse was lagging more than usual on the way home, I used the sight of The Goat to send Ned flying up the last hill, in the same manner that the sun's gravity is used to whip space probes around it and fling them toward the outer planets. It always worked with Ned, unless the neighbor's cows had jumped their fence and were lurking around the last bend. Then it was time to go into reverse. Other Ned peeves include garbage bags and plastic garbage cans set out curbside. Bridges, leaf piles, and any quick change of scenery (a grassy bank or a guardrail coming into view around a bend in the road) also make the list.

Cars and trucks, the usual concern of every horse driver because of their bad effect on the nerves of most equines, don't bother Ned in the least. He appears to be unaware of them. It seems to me you could maybe drive him down the middle lane of a city freeway and (not counting the obvious danger of being hit from behind) never experience a moment's concern—at least until Ned saw his first green-and-white directional sign overhead.

In retrospect, I can see where I went wrong in buying Ned from my Amish neighbor on Cherry Ridge. (Everyone within the bounds of one or two Amish church districts—maybe five square miles—is considered a neighbor and can expect to be included in weddings, funerals, and auctions.) He had purchased Ned a few months before "off the track," meaning the racetrack, point of origin for many of the driving horses used by plain people.

Ned, who never excelled enough to actually race,

started life as Specht's Strike and grew into a large and strong gelding, bay-colored, with a head as big and unwieldy as his given name. That awful head makes him a loser with standardbred fanciers. While he grew, he was trained to trot and pace pulling a two-wheeled cart. As my neighbor vouched, the future Ned apparently never showed any ability.

"He's too slow. That's why I'm selling him. He can go fast, but his heart isn't in it. He wants to slow down and look around too much."

Nevertheless, Ned had a point or two in his favor. He's a big, well-muscled horse, so I figured he could pull our heavy, old-fashioned wooden buggy up the steep hills in the Quaker community we intended to move to by summer's end. And my neighbor noted he was a "good traveler," meaning he can go long distances without unduly tiring.

We hitched him to the neighbor's buggy for a test drive and headed down the lane with his owner holding the driving lines. I'd never seen a horse before who let his tongue hang out the side of his mouth as he trotted. Between that and waving his head from side to side as he took in the scenery, he didn't look very intelligent.

I suggested we drive on the state highway to see how this horse handled alongside the steady stream of tourists and tractor-trailers. Actually, this choice must have relieved my neighbor, who seemed happy to prove his steed's mettle against engines rather than garbage bags and goats. Unfortunately, Ned showed his true colors before we made it onto the highway. At the stop sign he lifted his front half off the ground, then his backside, bronco style.

Now, if I had understood anything about horse trading, that would have been a good time to hop down and walk back home. But I didn't know anything, so off we went. Sure enough, Ned proved to have the most sought-after quality in a driving horse: He was "traffic-safe," at least when it came to the traffic itself. Whether it is safe to drive a horse whose goat phobia leads him to throw himself at oncoming cars from time to time is another matter. But the truth was that Ned was going cheap, and it was just as well that I bought him. Some of his mental problems and character defects can probably work themselves out as he matures. I have certainly learned a lot by driving him. He might make a fine eight-year-old. If, that is, he and I live that long.

You may at this point be asking yourself why anyone would be so stupid as to leave behind the comfort and convenience of the automobile for an unheated buggy pulled by a slow, neurotic horse. Why would I want to plod along at ten minutes to the mile, when a car can cover the same distance in sixty seconds? Those are reasonable questions, shared, I think, by many of the teenage Amish boys of our Holmes County neighborhood, a number of whom have a car stowed somewhere on the family premises.

The answers I am being given are still unfolding.

People in modern society already often express the desire to slow down their lives, so it probably isn't necessary for me to explain my desire to do the same. The fact that I don't want to get somewhere faster is understandable enough. But the idea that I am consciously limiting how far I want to be able to travel is hard for most non-plain people to fathom. How I achieve this limiting—having crazy Ned pull me in a big black wooden box on wheels, instead of riding a bike or calling a cab—is also contentious.

I receive frequent letters from a subscriber to the magazine I edit who thinks going the horse-and-buggy route is pretty silly. "Ride a bike!" he orders us from his home in northern California. Horses use up food. Bikes go farther and faster. People in the city can't use horses, so it isn't fair for us to.

I don't have anything against bicycles. In fact, I think they're the best invention of the Industrial Revolution. But when I read these letters, I wonder whether this guy has noticed that we're a family of five (soon to be six) people, living on a country road in a place that's under snow five months of the year.

A buggy is, for us, practical; it can carry us together, infants and all, through snow or rain. And the horse creates a connection with the world around us that I haven't sensed as clearly when pedaling a bicycle. A peculiar feeling of *yieldedness* as the animal submits to my control of the lines mixes with the sensation of the world's passing variety transmitted in the other direction, back up the harness to me, by the swings and bobs of his body and head.

Once I mastered some of Ned's quirks, there began to be some moments of calm between his incidents of skittishness. I discovered that any good-size hill kept Ned's mind on moving and off killing us both. During such moments I could look around and begin to have a traveling experience that closely paralleled that of walking.

A long, steep hill on the Ridge leading back home from

the blacksmith's shop, well beyond the range of my usual excursions on foot, adopted me into its place: the herd of steers on the far rise; the unusually small white horse barn with its gravel drive off to my right, a sorrel trotter poking her head out the top half of a Dutch door; lots of sun-warmed grass growing over well-tended swells and dips all the way up to the battered stop sign at the top of the hill.

It was on such trips I began to appreciate the old idiomatic expression "just passing through." Here was Ned, toiling at a walk up the hill, carrying me behind him with nary a notion of time or destination. Since he was pulling, I had deferred all such questions to him, and he wasn't interested in or even capable of answering them. We were indeed just passing *through*—through an infinite number of points and positions in a present reality, not going *to* so much as going *through*.

As Ned's behavior improved, I found that even when he was moving across flat earth at the powerful trot he occasionally musters, I never received the impression that we moved with any speed toward our destination. Far from it. We may have been moving just as swiftly as a rider on a bicycle, but the sensation for the driver of the buggy couldn't be more different.

The buggy's motion is a gentle tug forward, followed by a moment without any sense of movement; the wheels expend their momentum and then there is a slight feeling of falling back into the seat just as the next tug forward begins. Tug, hesitation, back. Each rocking movement is slightly different from the one that comes before it, as animal body and road coordinate. Surely this is how it feels to be a fetus carried in the womb. It is this impression of being carried by another living creature that imparts a serenity and feeling of presence no longer encountered in our modern adult world of travel.

Of course, if Ned is your beast of burden, it's best to be prepared to snap out of your reverie when he crests the hill and sees those cows milling about. Enjoy the view, but hold on to the reins.

Although I am trying to distinguish between horse power and the bicycle, I'm not faulting the latter. I'm just saying that every way of getting to somewhere gets you there differently. One thing bicycle travel does share with walking and driving a horse is that it doesn't objectify space the way faster modes of travel do. There is, I believe, a connection between pace—that is, distance covered divided by time—and the relationship we hold with our surroundings.

A moment ago, as I tried to write a description of what I "saw" as Ned traveled up the longest slope on the way home, I could only relate the externals: a white barn, some cows. The same description could be given from inside a car window, but with the buggy *something more was happening*. When I arrived home from such experiences, I arrived differently than when I rode the same route home in a car. I was affected. I carried something with me that stayed after the trip had ended. The only words I can think of that might describe what happened are *affection* and *responsibility*. At a slow pace, passing through a series of places and moments (instead of obliterating both place and moment with speed), I steadily come into relation with what I am seeing, hearing, perhaps touching, and smelling. It is such slow-time, real relationships that develop our ability to care, that speak to us and hold us responsible for the well-being of others outside ourselves. And we respond to this obligation (if we are open to receiving it) not with the modern tilt toward victimhood, whining over our loss of autonomy, but rather with affection. Love, even—for people, yes, but also for places, and for all the goodness God has given us to know and care for here.

When I am driving these days, I sometimes bring along preschool-age Jack. We take the old railroad bed route through a new forest that has grown up over recently abandoned farmland. The road is a deserted straightaway, and sometimes if Ned is behaving and I think it safe, we slow him to a walk and I hand the slackened driving lines to Jack. We lean against each other on the seat and talk, the buggy doors wide open and the stormfront (windshield) swung up and out of the way.

In the early fall, Jack notes the masses of wildflowers that bloom along the road bank, just below the tall, skinny maples. He correctly identifies the maples and daisies by their names. I point to a gap in the hillside that reveals a road down below us all the way at the bottom of the ridge, and I wonder aloud where it might lead.

Are we on our way somewhere? Or are we already here, *present,* lulled by the clip-clopping of hooves and the gently swaying buggy, yet also luminously aware and engaged with this moment?

I saw the last time I drove this route that sections of the hillside have been staked out for house lots. I would probably be happy about this if I drove a car and used the railroad bed as a shortcut to town. Good, now they'll pave this bumpy road and I can get there faster, I might think.

But I've come to love this quiet little path through the woods, because I have passed through it at its own pace. I know it. It obligates me to wonder if there is something I could or should do to help protect it from destruction.

Walking to Columbus reminds me that this obligation extends as far as my experience—direct experience—of the world does. Thinking of horse travel makes me pick up the pace set by my tapping staff. Here on this little-used section of the National Road is the cottage of a wood-carver. Some cobbled-together doghouses sit together nearest the road, but beyond them are dozens of intricately carved and painted figurines set out on the grass. Some are deeply imaginative renditions of everyday people. I have to stop and survey them all, laughing a little at the droller ones. How interesting this is. I almost want to walk the lane back to the garage I assume is his or her shop and see if I can strike up a conversation with the crafter of these images.

I suffer from PIG (post-image-glut) syndrome, so I have no desire to own any of these graven idols, mild as they are. However, I can't help but admire the skill and patience. Is it possible this person used to sell these in quantity to the many tourists and travelers who at one time took the Road, and continues to turn them out for a—presumably declining—buying public? I see, too, that whoever it is is not purely a regional folk artist. There are pop-culture fantasy figures mixed in with the personal creations, true modern cult idols: Snow White in her Disney incarnation, and others like her. Still, it is nice to stop and stand before the silent figures, who seem to benignly stare back at me. Could it be anything like this to glance out from a car?

My experience with driving Ned, frought with peril as it is, deepens my resolve to part with the privilege of operating a car. To become present, I feel I must give up as entirely as possible that quintessential means of obliterating places—the automobile.

I wish I could say that is all there is to it, a clean trade-off between a destructive technology and a healthy alternative. But the truth is that I have had to give up a lot of convenience. (And so has my wife, not without some regret.) We live in a country that is planned more or less exclusively for motor travel, which creates many, many difficulties for those choosing a slower mode.

Our family has been blessed with some aids to making the transition, aids that may be unavailable to others who want to follow our lead. We can call a cab if necessary to take us into town or to the doctor's office. I've been able up until now to travel by bus to a city where I could rent a car to take me on business trips, instead of having to hire a driver. Once my license is gone Mary Ann will still be a legal driver for a while longer—although, unlike me, she would never be willing to go through the rental hassle. None of these subsidies, however, has kept us from achieving our primary aim in releasing ourselves from the automobile, and we really have begun to regain a sense of place and belonging. Someday we may want to look back on both the difficulties and the blessings of this process and weigh them against each other. For now, however, Mary Ann and I—and our children—are content to let the complexities of this part of the simple life work themselves out.

A recent conversation with an Amish acquaintance bears out my experiences and helps me take heart as I walk the road today, on my way to giving up my license. A wheelwright and buggy maker by trade (as well as a farmer and sawmill operator), this staunchly conservative *Swartzentruber* Amishman was curious about our switch to horse power. No other Quakers in our Barnesville community drive horses—why do we?

I told him of my desire to regain a sense of place, and that I had become willing with the help of the Holy Spirit to trade some convenience for the privilege of becoming more responsible for the place where I live. At the time I thought that this explanation might be regarded as too intellectual, too "sensitive," for someone as practical as he to stomach.

A few days later, however, we were up at my barn discussing the reconstruction of the animal stalls and enclosures when he turned and said he had been considering my horse-and-buggy comment.

"I think you've got that just about right," he said slowly.

He told me that the Amish community depends in part on the limitations imposed by the horse. People have to rely on one another more when they are prevented from instantaneous mobility—which, of course, he thought was all to the good. For what would happen to the community if the members didn't have to rely on one another? What would happen to their trades if community members were easily drawn to shop outside the geographic boundaries of the church district? What would be the result for the community's future if teenage children had the unlimited power to run wherever they might?

Unlike the Amish, who make such limit-setting a group process, my transition to horse and buggy has necessitated a more individually sought loss of control, a limitation posed entirely from within rather than from without. But in both cases, of Amish *Ordnung* (ordering) or Quaker witness, the ultimate causal force is God. God is always asking us—as communities *and* individuals—to give up our willful control to Him.

I feel as if I am going to Columbus to give back the wider, shallower world I gained as an American citizen, age sixteen, when the keys to the car were first dropped into my hand. It has proven to be an illusory freedom. Losing control over where I can go puts me into a stronger relationship with people where I am—into a relationship of community.

This smaller world, which is slowly becoming as responsible for me as I am for it, provides a deeper and more authentic security, and therefore a greater freedom, than that of the wider, broader world in which I was handed a godlike control over time and space.

It occurs to me that this sense of security is something I have yet to fully apply to this trip to Columbus. I need to see that there isn't any destination for me on this earth. I'm just a few miles from Zanesville now, but why should I concern myself with whether I'm making good time today?

All of our speed betrays a hidden fear. Ned can be a scary beast of a driving horse, but I have to say that he has so far helped me find the one thing the wider world believes I have lost: freedom. Freedom to be one with my surroundings and to know that there is no earthly destination, that we're all just passing through.

It is past noon, and I haven't caught sight of Tasha and her brother. I don't have any food with me today, and the only restaurants and stores are at the highway interchanges. There are two fast-food restaurants up ahead. Standing inside one of them, I have to ask myself what would qualify as a healthy lunch in this environment. There are little nutrition-information booklets on the counter underneath a sign that says DID YOU KNOW? Glancing through one, I see that if we knew, we wouldn't eat here very often. Looking around at the other torsos in line and down at my own tells me that we don't need booklets to tell us this stuff isn't nutritious.

The cashier is a Mom. She calls back my order to the grill kid the way she would tell her son to pick up his dirty socks: "No meat on that! No meat at *all*, Tyler!"

It doesn't look right when it comes. It's in a cheeseburger wrapper, which is strange, but I take it anyway. Don't want to be a plain complainer. Salad, orange juice, french fries (400 calories, 250 of which are from fat). Still, I give thanks for it. I have a few miles to go yet, and I am grateful there is something for me to eat today.

Mom comes back to my table by the rear exit, a burger box in her hand, looking a little exasperated with Tyler as she tells me I have the wrong order; here's the no-meat one. But when she opens the little cardboard box there's a burger in it (575 calories, none of them slim). Mine doesn't have any meat on it, we discover when we unwrap it. The grill kid should have been trusted by both of us.

Speaking with her just serves to remind me that this is really a solitary trip. In that regard it is similar to a pilgrimage (although pilgrims to religious sites don't always, or even mostly, choose to make the approach singly). There is a No Loitering sign on the wall, so I am up and away. My feet are sore today, but they feel better after this brief rest.

Tasha and Jack are probably on their way home now from the play. I wonder if they remembered to sing today's song in morning devotion:

> There is a balm in Gilead
> to make the wounded whole
> There is a balm in Gilead
> to heal the sin-sick soul
>
> Some times I feel discouraged
> and think my work's in vain
> But then the Holy Spirit
> revives my soul again

It feels good to be outside, and to be singing. Off in the weeds I find an old milepost that hasn't been prettied up, and I stop to rest just for a moment and look at it. It sits on a small hillock, but because of the brush no one on the road can read its message: four miles to Zanesville.

Two miles farther to another rest. I just came down a

long grade along which was a bricked-in ditch, presumably from the National Road of World War I. Should I pry one up to bring home for Jack? That doesn't seem right, and, believe me, the guilt on an old historic preservationist's heart would be as heavy a load to lug home as would be the brick.

Now the road turns up—ever more steeply so. At the same time, Route 40 veers off to the south, and an even steeper road through the city's largest cemetery leads straight ahead. Without even thinking about it, I find myself slowly climbing the smooth black pavement of the cemetery road. This is the steepest hill of the trip so far. The still-bare trees are so large and close together throughout the cemetery that my walk is in the shade. It's almost dark going up this hill.

Now I shift into a lower gear. Or, to substitute a horse idiom, I put my shoulder to the plow, using my staff as another pair of horse legs. Now I'm Ned, just going up this hill moment by moment, no longer in control. I'm reciting my three beatitudes. Such a long, steep hill! But I do see a house or building at the top, so it isn't much more distant to the summit.

Losing control is partially what today's beatitude is about. William Barclay, in his commentary on the Gospel of Matthew, describes one of the meanings of the Greek word for "meek," as in:

Blessed are the meek:
for they shall inherit the earth

as

the regular word for an animal which has been domesticated, which has been trained to obey the
word of command, which has learned to answer to
the reins. It is the word for an animal which has
learned to accept control. So the second possible
translation of this beatitude is:

> Blessed is the man who has every instinct,
> every impulse, every passion under control.
> Blessed is the man who is entirely self-
> controlled.

The moment we have stated that, we see that it
needs a change. It is not so much the blessing of
the man who is *self*-controlled, for such complete
self-control is beyond human capacity; rather it
is the blessing of the man who is completely *God*-
controlled, for only in His service do we find our
perfect freedom, and in doing His will our peace.

I feel that perfect freedom as I crest the hill. I hear a
silent Whoa! and I stop and look all around. I am at the
highest point of the city, from which I can see all of
Zanesville stretching down toward the Muskingum River.
I've come fifty miles on foot from my home, by the grace
of God.

The Fourth Day

*Blessed are they which do hunger and thirst
after righteousness: for they shall be filled.*

I've woken up in another motel room bed, feeling about
the best I have so far on this journey. After hearing from
the children on the telephone about their play, I dropped
off almost immediately and got in a good ten hours of
sleep. Sitting at the faux wood table in my room, I'm catching up my journal about yesterday's travels.

This is the twelfth day of Fourth Month. It's a Saturday; in plain speech, a Seventh Day. Although I don't
choose to claim this day for Saturn, I do acknowledge that
it signifies the beginning of the weekend. And it is the
fourth day of my trip. And it is raining.

Breakfast is available in the lobby, and I head there after putting some clothes in the motel's coin-operated washing machine.

A large bus tour group has formed a line in the lobby.
These folks seem extremely well groomed—perhaps I'm
noticing their immaculate qualities more than I otherwise

would because I feel self-conscious in my scruffy plain pilgrim garb.

The clothes will take a while to wash, so I have some time to spend while the bus tourists stand in their line. They are going to the big pottery factory up the road, one of them tells another, who looks a bit bored by this news. In fact, a scan of their faces reveals everyone is bored. What do people do on bus tours? From the looks of what people are carrying onto the bus, the answer is shopping.

The ladies (and a few men) begin to move forward and board their bus. The look of them reminds me of a train ride our family took to nowhere, soon after I began to grow more confident in driving Ned. (Ned was as object-phobic as ever, prancing along the byways into oncoming traffic at the sight of any object—animate or not—next to the road.)

We were finally able to travel together as a family because I had learned to handle him—how the driving lines could hold his head forward and how to make him mind. My friend Marvin took Ned and me on a few wild rides through the dusty gravel roads along Goose Bottom, teaching me how to get Ned's attention back on me, where it belonged.

"Watch his ears!" Marvin directed. Sure enough, they spun around like little periscopes, and when neither one was "looking" back at me, it meant Ned's attention was focused elsewhere—on the next scary mailbox up ahead, for instance.

Among their own kind, horses determine who is going to take orders from whom—dominance—by wickedly biting each other on the rump. Marvin's method was identical, except he substituted less painful taps with a whip and a bellow of "Listen to me, Ned!" that warned the cows ahead of our rapid approach. Ned started listening.

"That was pretty good," said Marvin in his lugubrious Holmes County accent. We had just careened into his driveway after another hair-raising run through the dust. "That might be the fastest he's ever trotted."

Yes, indeed.

I was also learning to outsmart Ned by changing the scenery on him. I discovered that his good behavior on the highway "test drive" before I bought him wasn't a fluke. He really did travel better on the main road than on all the little back ways I had tried to sneak him down. The relatively few distractions on either side of the state highway meant I could spend less time averting disasters. I could go to Sugarcreek, run errands, and make it back home before lunch. I started taking one or the other of the two older children along on my newly safer trips.

Late in Seventh Month of that year, our family prepared to emerge from our Amish country refuge. In the time before we made the move to Barnesville we wanted to give our children a chance to say goodbye. Part of our Holmes County leavetaking involved a promised ride on the excursion railroad line that runs from Sugarcreek—the "tourist train," as it was locally known.

Little Tasha and Jack had heard the train's faraway whistle all summer, reminding them of the big black engine, puffing out steam and smoke, that they had seen next to the depot. Mary Ann and I decided to make a ride on the train the first full family outing by way of the buggy.

The morning of our trip dawned into brilliant sunshine, and we were up early to prepare. Soon we were sitting together and moving to the smooth lunges of Ned's powerful body as the surrey rolled up the steep dirt road toward Highway 39. Mary Ann sat to the left of me with babe Suze in her arms (buggy drivers, unlike those in automobiles, sit on the right—perhaps better to eye the ditches a buggy might fall into). Jack and Tasha sat behind us on a low wooden bench. No seat belts: If a car hits your buggy, your best hope is to be thrown clear. As we rounded the L-shaped dogleg turn at the top of the hill, Ned lurched a bit onto the berm. What now? I wondered.

Someone had cut hay across the road and left the square bales in the field. Add them to the phobia list. Ned charged on toward the highway. At the stop sign, Mary Ann had a sudden thought—was this garbage day in Sugarcreek? Because if this was indeed the day of the week the good people of Sugarcreek wheel out to the curb their hundreds of identical green garbage cans, we were sunk. Plastic garbage cans bother Ned's disturbed brain almost as much as do goats. The last time I drove Ned through town on garbage day the cans lined both sides of the road, and he took off at a gallop.

But there was no need to worry; it was a different day of the week, and the roadsides were clear. We were safe.

Turning onto this particular highway is never a problem, and driving Ned on it is almost carefree. Despite the heavy traffic of tourists and semi trucks, there is little to watch out for, Ned-wise. The road has an extra-wide paved berm and a gravel apron beyond that, which together make up the "buggy lane." This road alongside the road allows motor vehicles to pass us without having to cross the dividing line into oncoming traffic.

At the first traffic light in Sugarcreek we veered onto a more residential street down into town, and there we encountered our only real mishap of the day. Ahead on the right an elderly man stood trimming his curbside hedge, dropping the clippings into . . . *his green plastic garbage can.*

Well, there it was. Would Ned see it? What would he do?

Nothing happened as we passed; we think he hasn't seen it—but suddenly his head whips to the side and then he dashes in the opposite direction, into the path of a desperately swerving pickup truck.

How close was it? It turns out that nobody knows for sure because we all shut our eyes and screamed at the same time. "Dog food!" I whispered at him under my breath.

Trotting downhill on Main Street into the village proper, I turned Ned to the right onto Factory Street, and then into the enormous buggy parking lot hidden behind the storefronts on Main. Here two long hitching rails each tether a dozen horses and rigs. The local plain folk congregate back here in small droves: men, women, and children coming and going in their somber-colored clothes, or stopped in conversation with neighbors and friends.

On my visits to this place the squared-off corners of my Quaker buggy always won the recognition of those

Amish who knew our family, and startled looks from those who didn't. What to make of us? We weren't the "English" (non-Amish locals), and we weren't the tourists, but we sure weren't Amish (as anyone would know who could read the secret language of buggy shapes and coat-collar designs). No, we were definitely odd. However, I guess our similarities to the Amish were enough to make us approachable from their point of view, and approached we were. A few minutes of explanatory conversation always led to new friendships.

At such times I often thought of the hundreds of tourists milling about on the other side of the wall of shops along Main, kin to the bus tourists I'm watching ride off from the motel in Zanesville. The Sugarcreek tourists were poking their heads into the Amish Country T-Shirt Factory and the Swiss Village Bakery, fingering the knick-knacks crammed on the shelves of Country Corn and Stuff or in the more upscale L'Heritage Collection—hoping, I would guess, to spy among the little Amish figurines some of the rather elusive Amish of flesh and blood.

But no Amish person sets foot inside these places, as either buyer or seller. The functional shops on Main, like Spector's fabric store, have back entrances facing the hitching rail piazza. The black-bonneted Amish matrons and their relatives slip in and out of these places, hardly seen as they go about their errands.

If Main Street is a sort of a wall, it is nevertheless a wall around which anyone, any *tourist*, might freely walk. Physically there is no barrier between the tourists and the world they seek to visit. Very few, however, do come around to our side. It is as if, having been trained all their lives to answer every yearning with a purchase, they can no longer formulate another route to answering their curiosity about the plain people.

If the tourists have come here looking for the Amish, and for the road America turned off so many years ago, it must be said that they leave instead with nothing but a bag full of things, "stuff." I doubt the bag holds any satisfaction or contains any comfort for the underlying need. As is so often the case for people today. I think again of the bored expressions on the faces of the Zanesville bus tourists.

How frustrating it must be to set out on a journey where one has been promised a bracing experience (the side of the tour bus parked outside the Gospel Shop in Sugarcreek proclaims that an unforgettable "Amish Odyssey" awaits), only to end up in the Swiss Village on Main Street. It is a place only as real as Santa's Wonderland down at the mall.

Say a prayer that more of us will hear the Lord calling us away from these places and into more meaningful pursuits.

Of course, those of us behind Main Street weren't exactly holding a prayer meeting all this time. Like all the others along the hitching rails, we had errands to run (plus a train to catch), so we needed to move quickly. I had brought my good boots to be repaired—now the Saddle and Shoe Shop had to substitute for Yoder's back up in Geauga County. I fished them out of the back of the surrey after tying up Ned and helping Mary Ann step down.

Then we were off and running: "Here, let's split up—I'll take Jack and buy our tickets. You and Tasha and Suze drop off my library books and meet me at the blacksmith's bench by the shoe shop." Then off to the pharmacy and back to the buggy to look in on Ned before the train leaves.

Ned was already half asleep on his feet when we came back to check on him. Before we'd left home he had eaten a big meal of oats and drained his water bucket, so he would likely remain contented for another hour or two while we were gone. He stood with his eyes closed and tongue still splayed out the side of his face, as it had been all the way to town. Looking at him, I could almost forgive him for putting us all in harm's way. I took a moment to gently stuff his tongue back into his mouth. "Hold thy tongue, Ned!" I mock-scolded him in a whisper as the children turned red with laughter.

The tourist train is actually a short piece of what was formerly the Baltimore and Ohio (B&O) rail lines; these tracks once carried the freight from Cleveland to Zanesville, where I am now on my walk to Columbus. The B&O wiped out the canal boat business of the early 1800s with its superior speed. The B&O was taken over eventually by Norfolk and Western, which then began losing freight to interstate highway trucking in the 1950s. Today a small company ekes a profit from the Cleveland to Youngstown freight run, along with this small excursion line.

Walking between the depot and the train, the children's eyes widened as they got a close-up look at engine no. 51, a gold-trimmed black behemoth hooting and hissing as it was "getting up the steam" to make the ten-mile trip to the village of Baltic and back. The train's engineer, who was dressed in blue coveralls and a striped cap, tested the screaming air brakes. We hurried to our place in the line of tourists waiting to board.

The rail cars were an assortment of early-twentieth-century passenger compartments painted over with the black and yellow colors of the excursion line. Ahead of us a Mennonite congregation nearly filled one of the cars. Meanwhile, Jack and Tasha leaped up and down with the excitement of being in a crowd. The shadow of the smoke rising from the train engine's stack was passing across the sun-baked gravel next to the platform.

Mary Ann and I exchanged looks. I knew that she, like me, was beginning to wonder if we had made a mistake bringing the children here. It was supposed to be an educational experience for them, but most of those in line clearly regarded the train as an amusement, something on the order of a carousel ride at the county fair.

The noontime sun beat down on us as the line began moving again. An intense feeling of alienation began to grow in my gut as I stood there in a crowd of my fellow Americans. It's a curious thing, this sensation that I've experienced in public places all of my adult life. And it had only grown stronger in that year spent among the very, very modestly dressed and (mostly) physically fit Amish of Holmes County. The differences in behavior and appearance encountered in the larger world have come to seem ever more amazing and bizarre.

Standing at separate points in line, two large men, both

sunburned and wearing similar T-shirts and Bermuda shorts, were panning their video cameras back and forth at the train—and at us. Looking over the crowd, my thoughts alternated between the reminder to love thy neighbor as thyself (we must, after all, look a little different and funny to our Amish neighbors) and the fearful realization that we live in the midst of a soft and pleasure-seeking people.

Have mercy, O Lord, on me, also a sinner.

For good or ill, the change to horse and buggy has sheltered us. Leading a sheltered life is no longer considered a positive thing, for either children or adults. One should get out into the world and experience it! Strange as it may seem, the sheltered life we have chosen actually informs us much better about this world we are expected to embrace without any forethought. As in Mary Ann's parable of the counterfeit-money detectors, we have been looking at the real thing over and over again. We have been living a bracingly authentic existence within the confines of a plain life, and it has made us wiser. It has enabled us to recognize—at least sometimes—the false and the empty when we venture forth.

Wisdom doesn't confer superiority, however. Thinking I am one up on people is a trap that leads back to isolation and self-loathing. Jesus tells us in the Bible that we will be judged in heaven by the measure with which we judge others here on earth. To the contrary of feeling wise, I felt a little foolish and embarrassed to have brought my children into a carnival-like atmosphere when we spend so much time at home emphasizing sobriety.

High-pitched, unripe laughter and profanity peppered

the conversations around us in the line as we boarded. But the children noticed none of that, thankfully; they were busy looking all around at the inside of the rail car, at the antique electric light fixtures and slide-up windows. Outside on the gravel, the portly, smiling conductor in his yellow-trimmed uniform helped passengers board the train. The last passengers put on were an urban couple and their young son. Steam shot from the engine ahead and with a whiff of coal smoke and a *toot-toot* of the whistle, the train slowly left the station.

We chugged across Main Street and past the Goshen Dairy store, where a man videotaped our departure from Sugarcreek. Inside the train a public-address speaker crackled to life and an unseen announcer in one of the other cars asked, "Do any of you know which state has the most Amish?"

Mary Ann and I exchanged worried looks again. I'd assumed the attraction of the excursion train lay in its old-time way of traveling. But now it appeared we were in for a tour of "Amish country." Without intending it, we'd come around to the other side of the wall separating the plain people from the tourists.

The tour guide's voice continued, a burbling combination of reasonably true facts about the Amish (they plow with horses) and some bad jokes (Q: Why do they raise oats? A: To feed their Oatsmobiles. That one had Tasha laughing).

"There on the right is the Sugarcreek livestock sale barn. When it burned down a few years ago, the Amish rebuilt it in a day. . . . That little building by the road isn't an outhouse. It's a telephone booth. . . ."

Yes, it was. And I knew the owner of that house, that stable. It hadn't occurred to me that this train ride to nowhere was actually a tour of my neighbors' backyards. Cameras pointed out the windows and clicked.

"To the Amish there are two types of folks: Amish, meaning them, and English, meaning everybody else."

Several people looked at us, I noticed. Here we were, my plainly dressed wife and I clutching our young, beginning to feel something like a family of giraffes riding the African safari tour bus.

"There's a typical Amish farm on the left. Note the smaller home beside the large, white farmhouse. That's the dawdy-grandpa house. The Amish keep their old people at home. They don't believe in retirement communities." The elderly couple seated in front of us nodded.

"Taking care of family goes back to their tradition of caring for one another. They don't believe in taking government help like Social Security."

Up on a far hill we saw a field with little white headstones, an Amish cemetery I'd gone past in my travels with Ned. Nearer the track was Rush Run School.

"There's an Amish school on your right. It's a one-room school with as many as twenty-five pupils. They're let out of school in April. They have no snow days and only five holidays. The schoolhouse has no indoor plumbing, so the water is carried in from that pump.

"Holmes County has the lowest unemployment rate, the

lowest crime rate, and the lowest divorce rate in Ohio. . . ." Passengers on both sides craned their necks to see the exotic inhabitants of a horse-drawn open wagon traveling the road in the opposite direction the train was moving.

Watching the horse's legs flash up and down, time stopped for a moment, and in the silence I asked myself who was more exotic, this somberly dressed couple quietly driving their wagon to market, or the neon-suited strangers pointing at them from the train. That was, I suppose, a nonsensical question, because it is a matter of perspective and opinion.

Perhaps it would be a more useful query to ask one another what we really require for a contented life. The people on the train, whatever their present condition, are seeking, searching for the answer. It may be that this exposure to the Amish, who seem tranquilly assured in their way of living, will be of significant help—even if it only causes the searcher to begin doubting that he or she heretofore has been looking in the right places.

The jollity of the train ride made it impossible for us to dig into the deep questions with our fellow passengers. In many other situations, however, we've had wonderful openings—opportunities—to talk with people who are in the mainstream. Always we try to impart a historical perspective on our newfound way of life: The twentieth century has been an era in which limitations were dissolved. In the previous centuries, people lived with many limitations. They drove horses. They received nothing from the government. They sent their children to one-room schools.

If those on the train could take away one idea from

what they heard about and saw of the Amish, I hoped it would be this one: *This is how it once was, and could be again.*

When the train stopped on a side rail at Baltic, no one got off but the engineer. The passengers stood in the aisles and flipped the seatbacks around to face the opposite direction, while the engineer brought his steam engine up to the other end of the train. Sitting down again with Tasha, Jack, and baby Susanna on our laps, Mary Ann and I were prepared for the trip back to where we'd begun. With a hiss of the brakes and a slight lurch to one side, the train resumed its trip, the tour guide launching into a description of Amish worship practices.

I was ready to get back to Sugarcreek and the hitching rail where my horse stood in a dream with his tongue hanging out. Ready especially for the slow, and possibly dangerous, trip back to our home, driving Ned.

So much about my life at home rewards me with its slowness that reveals the texture and depth of life. There are no sounds in the house but the sounds made by people. Mary Ann likes structure, and there is an unhurried but certain pace to the day's activity: animal chores, breakfast, recorder practice, household chores, school (Bible story, Bible verses, narration, writing, history, math), a snack, and the late morning break. During the break all three children tend to clump together onto the couch. They like to read and be read to. Jack, although he himself can't read, can at least show two-year-old Susanna the pictures in the Bible storybook and let her tell him what they mean.

"Oh, Jack, tat's Eve. She pickin' the fruit from the tree of *bad* and *evil!*"

Sometimes we stay home from meeting and have our own silent worship in the living room. There is deep satisfaction to be found in sitting quietly for an hour with a calm and silent child leaning back against you. It takes some learning, but even Susanna can mostly stay in the profound stillness. At home, the ministry that occurs is usually in the form of singing, soft hymns on which we all often join in. But most of the time is spent in a richer quiet than may ever be experienced by many people today. It lends a texture and reality to our lives, and is a blessed replacement for the irreal, virtual life of career, commute, consume that Mary Ann and I have given up.

A cold drizzle is falling on Zanesville. Outside the motel lobby's plate-glass windows the tour bus rumbles away in the rain, on its way to the pottery factory. As soon as it's gone I put my clothes in the dryer in the little laundry room and head back upstairs to finish up in my journal and begin getting ready for today's leg of the trip.

The clock radio in my room is blaring out country music; the previous, apparently late-sleeping tenant must have left the alarm set. Earlier I took each item from the pack and laid it on the bed. Now I need to consider how best to repack. While I do so the clock radio on the bedstand continues to make itself known, digitally clicking back and forth between time and date: 10:01, 4-12, over and over.

A year ago on this day I was in a car driving to Barnesville to finish preparations for the Second Luddite Congress, scheduled to begin the next day. We were expecting a lot of people. Most of them were folks who were at the point Mary Ann and I had reached when we had Tasha:

They were looking for alternatives to the technosphere of modern life, to the digital clock ticking away their existence in a mechanistic fashion. A lot of them were subscribers to *Plain* magazine. There were also a good number of Mennonites and Amish and some Brethren coming, more out of solidarity than out of a need to learn more.

The name of the conference was invented from a snippet of history involving the original Luddite movement in early-nineteenth-century England. The Luddites held a "First Congreſſ" of their numbers in 1812. It was at a time when the Industrial Revolution had just begun, but had already sparked a tremendous rebellion. Independent weavers of cloth and all manner of "cottage" (read "home") manufacturers openly resisted the destruction of their way of life caused by the newly introduced factory system and automated machinery. These Luddite tradesmen began to burn factories to the ground and break up the new machinery.

Before the congress they had never engaged in violence against people. There was even an element of humor to their rebellion: They delighted in baffling the government and its spies with a fictional leader from whom they pretended to receive their orders, General Ned Ludd.

The truth was that they were a popular uprising against the machine age. Their early successes in vandalizing factories made it look for a brief moment as if they might stop the Industrial Revolution in its tracks.

Just as the English troops prepared to mount a concerted attack, the Luddites met in their congress to discuss tactics—and to plan a "Second Congreſſ."

Their decision was to escalate the violence and fight back against the English troops. For money and arms, they would turn to banditry. They quickly lost public sympathy. Within a few months, the soldiers and their allies, the factory owners, wiped the Luddite movement from the face of the earth. The "Second Congress" was never held, and meaningful resistence to modernity never again materialized.

Feeling some sympathy and kinship with the initial sentiment—though not the actions—of the original Luddites, I organized the Second Luddite Congress on behalf of *Plain* magazine in the hope we could steer the question of how to resist in a new direction from where it was headed when the Luddites last gathered together. If we could develop a tactic of peaceful "nonresistant resistance" as a group that was based on the kinds of things Mary Ann and I had been doing in our own lives, maybe we could succeed where the Luddites had failed.

I went into the congress with a lot of hope, and that hope has carried me along even here to Zanesville. I need to be grateful that it is hope that makes this journey with me, instead of violence. I need to continue traveling in a mindful, deliberate fashion.

A quick check out the window tells me that I had better prepare carefully for today's walk, even though it is one of the shorter ones on the itinerary—only about thirteen miles. Sweatshirt, coat, poncho. The only place open to buy food this morning is a sandwich shop, so I get one for lunch and put another in my pack for supper down the road.

After a mile it turns out that Route 40 is closed where an old bridge has been knocked down to prepare for the building of a new one. Cars are being shuttled onto the interstate, but I can't go that way. A man at a gas station confirms that it isn't possible to walk through the construction, but he earnestly figures out a walking route for me that will get me past the downed bridge. A side street takes me in a loop underneath the interstate, then through a modest neighborhood along Rehl Street. I had thought when he gave me the directions back at the gas station that it was "Real Street" I was looking for, which made a certain amount of sense, since it leads me back to the realest of streets, the National Road. Now I've walked about two miles, and Route 40 finally comes into view at the bottom of a steep drop in the road.

This section of the Road is a divided four-lane expressway, roaring with weekend traffic, cars and trucks in equal measure. As I look west, the travel looks to be basically uphill at a low incline for the next five miles or more. I'm blessed, however, with a bike lane all to myself. It's wider even than the buggy lane on the state route where I took Ned for his test drive. I have it all to myself, since today's travelers are all mounted on their engined beasts.

The buggy lane in Sugarcreek was actually built as a bike path. The government was at first petitioned by the county to provide the use of bike path funds to build the buggy lane, but the Department of Transportation was emphatic: Bike path construction could occur only if the county met the required condition of having a certain number of bike riders. No counting horses.

But it so happened that the Amish of Holmes County also ride bikes to and from their outside jobs (many other Amish districts ban the use of bicycles). There are a lot more adult riders in that part of Holmes County (and over into Tuscarawas County, which the village of Sugarcreek is actually in), more than in any other rural county in the state. So the bike path was built. Only someone, somehow, forgot to mark it as a bike path—the one I'm walking on has Bikes Only painted on its surface every few feet—and without that designation it is naturally regarded as primarily a buggy lane. You can still ride your bike on the Sugarcreek bike path, but you have to keep your eyes peeled to avoid running over what the horses leave behind.

The going is easy, and my staff is again superfluous. The only thing I need to remember to do is to hold on to my hat when the trucks sweep by me. After a while it begins to rain off and on, so I take the poncho out of the pack. There's little to see or remark on in today's scenery. The blandness imposed by the constructed space that surrounds the expressway on both sides, along with the boring safety of my smooth bike path, makes this part of my walk difficult in a new way. There's a gracelessness to the re-rendering of the landscape for the sake of convenience. A lot gets lost: human-size scale, proximity to nature, any sense of variety or texture underfoot. I'd like to find the engineer and take him on a tour of my homestead, where we are trying to apply the values that were factored out of the bike route.

Even in the short time we've been in Barnesville, Mary Ann and I have regained our connection to nature—our literal dependence on the sun and the rain. Our personal care for our household and the land has the goal of closing the energy loop and existing within the sun's budget of light falling on our three acres of house, gardens, woods, barn, and small pasture. To make all these things work together with nature demands a certain diminution of our needs, so that we are in balance, at the right scale with nature.

Instead of burning up the world with cars and coal-fired electricity, we've sworn off gas and oil and opted out of the electric grid. Instead of pouring carbon into the air, we're taking a lot out of the atmosphere through the growing of trees. There are many more trees growing on our small homestead than on the average suburban lot of similar size. Two pine copses on either side of the lane leading to the house and barn were planted forty years ago by the tree-loving previous tenant; there are numerous forty- and fifty-foot-tall maples, chestnuts, hemlocks, and blue spruces on the hillside leading down from the barn, as well as a small sugar maple grove of twelve fifty-foot trees at the end of our tiny horse pasture. We've planted a small peach orchard, too, as well as some individual fruit trees and bushes to replace ornamental plantings.

We call this place Arbor Hill, and it all sounds very wonderful, but the truth is that in most cases I haven't really known what I was doing—or what I was getting myself into—when I've taken steps to prepare this spot for a more sustainable future. At the end of the job of building a huge three-part compost bin at the edge of the lower woods, I could only stand back, sigh, and know that I could do a much better job next time—if, that is, I ever have another chance. From the spindly and leaning appearance of my construction efforts, that chance may well come soon. It's as graceless as the bike path, but in a different way.

Other projects have gone better the first time, though usually at a slower pace than I would like. It took all fall and winter to turn the "garage," a spacious thirty feet by twenty feet, back into the livestock barn it once was. Now it is winterized and houses Ned and some goats, as well as assorted horse- and human-powered vehicles and machines.

The lawn gets mowed by the horse, pulling a gang mower composed of three old-fashioned reel mowers bolted together to make a wider cut than is possible with a large riding mower. I walk behind it with a set of extra-long lines to control the horse. Very fast and exciting lawn care, and the horse's hooves aerate the soil.

Our extensive, newly plowed garden plots (Ned couldn't be trusted, so we had a tractor do it) have taken over large parts of the front and side yards. The peach orchard, high-bush cranberries, and blueberry hedges are all within view of the kitchen window. When I look out the glass and see all this beauty and fertility, all the husbandry side by side with nature on a formerly farmed-out scrap of Appalachian hillside, I believe I am seeing a vision of what could happen to all those suburban lots that have given the natural world and the human soul so much heartache.

Our house is small, really more of a cottage than a home for five-going-on-six people. We light the night with a few gas lamps, and we power our water heater and refrigerator with propane. Since we don't have an automobile, these two items account for most of our fossil-fuel use.

Here on our hill the northern winds of winter are cold. We heat with an old, water-jacketed wood furnace retrofitted to warm the existing baseboard radiators. Sam, a self-described "old Quake" hippie, did a lot of the work of getting the heavy old furnace down into the basement with a come-along and some pallet jacks. While we were lowering it down the cement steps, it ripped several light switches off the wall next to it, and Sam shouted down to me from his position by the winch: "You don't need those anymore, anyway, do you?"

With the addition of some new basement pipes, it was ready to go. Where an electric pump and fuel-oil burner once provided the hot-water heat, now fallen trees and snags from the community's property heat the water, which naturally expands and pushes through the radiators without need for any pumps.

The water for our heating system and most of our other household needs flows down from a cistern by the barn, where runoff from the barn roof is captured and filtered. The run down the hill creates enough pressure for most uses, but I haven't yet rigged up a viable shower in the bathroom. I've tried a lot of shower-like inventions in the bathtub, cheap kits from the hardware store. Jack's comment about the one that attached to the faucet and kept coming loose was right on target: "Dad, this doesn't actually work, does it?" Drinking water and water for cooking come from a well that we are in the process of changing over to a wind- and solar-powered pump.

What we are doing in our small way is to heal the split between culture and nature through a return to careful and meaningful agriculture, domesticity, and husbandry. Exploring the question of how we might come to preserve nature in its wild state (that is, to let it be), we have to work with it a little, at least until we learn the lesson that what we do to or for nature we also visit upon ourselves. Writer and farmer Wendell Berry calls this lesson the knowing of the limits of our self-interest:

> In the recovery of culture *and* nature is the knowledge of how to farm well, how to preserve, harvest, and replenish the forests, how to make, build, and use, return and restore. In this *double* recovery, which is the recovery of our humanity, is the hope that the domestic and the wild can exist together in lasting harmony.

On Arbor Hill we are far from achieving our goals, far from perfect in engaging in this marvelous recovery project. We haven't approached it grandly; we've done it on the cheap—even practically for nothing. We have been blessed with frugal predecessors, country people who left us many of the things that a modern homesteader should expect to have to furnish for him- or herself, such as the cistern and the trees.

I don't know the beliefs that motivated those who tended Arbor Hill before we came to it, but Mary Ann and I have approached our caring for it as a way of trusting God and looking for His righteousness to prevail, not our own more limited sense of what is right. This single-minded pursuit of God—what a Quaker might call the emptying out of self-righteousness—is a potent refutation of the modern call to self-fulfillment.

Blessed are they which do hunger and thirst after
righteousness: for they shall be filled.

The entire Sermon on the Mount turns on this powerful beatitude like a wheel around its axle. In every verse that follows, Jesus describes the life that wills itself to be filled with God's righteousness, the life lived for self, and the eternal consequences of each:

Let your light so shine before men, that they may see
your good works, and glorify your Father which is in
heaven. (Matthew 5:16)

For I say unto you, That except your righteousness shall
exceed that of the scribes and Pharisees, ye shall in no
case enter into the kingdom of heaven. (5:20)

But seek ye first the kingdom of God, and His righteous-
ness; and all these things shall be added unto you.
(6:33)

Jesus warns us not to be self-righteous, not to judge, not to be a hypocrite. But He also brings us a wonderful promise that there is truly a way to be filled with God's righteousness.

The people who planned and built this bikeway and expressway did a good job within their understanding of what is needed to make travel "work," but they forgot to consider the human side of *how* we go places. Likewise, there are many people who sit in church on Sunday with the intention of worshiping God, yet they see no connection between their daily walk—all the decisions about how to live that we make from moment to moment—and worship. If our hearts are set single-mindedly on the Lord, then worship and life are the same thing. On earth as it is in heaven, amen.

The rain has let up a lot, but a colder wind is blowing my hat off my head whenever a semitrailer roars by too close to my "easy" path. Fortunately, I have just about reached a turnoff that will put me on a more rural and tree-lined road that runs parallel to the main line. The road is even steeper than the six miles or so of uphill climb I've already negotiated, but the views are beautiful. It seems as if the land here has almost totally regrown its original tree cover. I slow my walking to a lower gear, and the buckeye walking staff becomes a climbing tool.

The incline levels off into the small, mostly poverty-stricken town of Mount Sterling. I pause to eat my sandwich on the steps of the little Methodist church in the center of town, sharing some scraps with a neighborhood terrier. It is definitely getting colder. Maybe it's partly the elevation; I must be several thousand feet higher above sea level than when I left Zanesville. Putting on my gloves, I start off in a hurry; I am only a mile or two, I guess, from tonight's destination.

The walking is easier, and I can reflect some more on how Mary Ann and I ended up in a religious denomination that so strongly emphasizes a daily "dying to self."

I know that each of us was "pushed" when we made our individual leaps of faith. We shared a growing alienation from the fast-moving, self-propelled world around us. It is probably not so amazing that we should be drawn to the Friends, since it was just such feelings that spurred the origins of that religious movement centuries ago.

George Fox, the founder of the Friends, had his own pivotal moment in his long journey toward a personal relationship with the Living God in the same context of alienation. He relates in his *Journal* that he had a life-changing experience while on an errand of business that took him to an English fair. He was almost nineteen years old at the time, a sensitive and religiously inclined boy. He ran into one of his cousins, a Puritan a little older than himself, whom George respected for his religiosity. With him was a companion, and they asked George to join them for a jug of beer at the alehouse there at the fair.

And I, being thirsty, went in with them; for I loved any that had a sense of good, or that sought after the Lord. When we had drunk each a glass, they began to drink healths, calling for more, and agreeing together that he that would not drink should pay all. I was grieved that any who made profession of religion should do so . . . wherefore I rose up to go, and putting my hand into my pocket, laid a groat on the table before them, and said, "If it be so, I will leave you." So I went away.

He went, in fact, as one biographer puts it, "out of the inn, out of the fair, out of his job and out of his home—in search of a faith which would really show itself in the lives of those who professed it."

I wonder what he would think about my walk to Columbus.

I called a local church a few weeks ago to ask if there was anyone willing to take an overnight lodger, briefly explaining my trip. I was given the name and address of a woman on this road with a spare room who is willing to let me use it tonight. It isn't hard to find her home, and after a ring of the electric doorbell a kind-looking woman in her early fifties answers and invites me in. Something makes me leave my stick by the door.

Her home is warm and colorful. There are many ceramic pots made in the style of the pottery factory on the bus tour's itinerary from this morning. ("My son works there," my hostess tells me when I comment on them.) She sees me glance over to a collection of photographs on top of the TV console, and she lovingly catalogs for me her children and their children and stepchildren. The absence of a deceased husband's picture tells me she is divorced. Looking around again, I can see that she must live here all alone except for her cat.

We talk for a few minutes about my trip and about her

work, which involves computers. Her kindness reaches across past the differences in our lives. As has been usual on this trip, I feel the need to maintain my solitude, even though it would be nice to have a long conversation after four days of self-imposed virtual silence. But after a while I ask if I could go somewhere to rest.

My room, where I finally get to slough off my heavy pack, is nicely made up and done in calmer hues than the downstairs. My back hurts enough that as soon as I am alone I have to lie down, and there I stay for at least an hour. Staring at the ceiling, I remember to sing today's song softly to myself, the song my wife and children probably sang around the big cherry table at breakfast today. I can see them, their sweet faces alive against the backdrop of plain walls and wooden floors in the long, bare open space at the center of our home.

> Consider the lilies of the field
> They neither toil nor spin
> Yet I tell you that even Solomon
> Was not arrayed like these.
>
> What shall we eat, Lord?
> What shall we drink?
> What shall we put on to wear?
>
> Is not life more than food?
> The body more than clothes?
> Consider the lilies of the field
> They neither toil nor spin.

It's about time to go back downstairs and indulge in a little more conversation. On the silk-striped wall next to my bed I have been looking at a large framed print of a Victorian painting. In it a very young girl sits in solitude on a rock. She looks a little lonely, though her features are relaxed, quiet, and childlike in every way. A small cat is cuddled in her lap.

After eating some generously proffered fruit and talking some more with my benefactress, I hobble back upstairs. It's nine o'clock. Pressing my face against the cold glass of the window beside my bed and looking out into the darkness, I can see that it has begun to snow.

The Fifth Day

Blessed are the merciful: for they shall obtain mercy.

I'm up at five-thirty. The wind is throwing cold, dry snowflakes against the dark window of my room. Feeling around for my clothes, I begin to ready myself and my backpack, pulling out extra layers of clothing and straightening what remains in the pack. Today is Sunday—First Day, I would say—and the owner of the house is asleep. Slipping quietly downstairs, I make my breakfast from the things that have been left out for me. I had been offered a home-cooked breakfast, but I wanted to get an early start back on the road.

The emptiness of these rooms in the morning light makes me miss my family. Even though we don't really have any decorations, our home always seems so full to me. We sleep piled into just two rooms, both of which open out onto the large main room that is a living area at one end and a dining area at the other, about thirty-five feet by twenty, I think. Life continually springs out of one of the surrounding rooms in the form of a child, possibly Susanna pulling her wooden duck on wheels behind her, or Jack clutching an old handmade nail he's found up by the barn, or Tasha bringing a book over to the morning light in the playroom.

Before I can leave today there's a final hurdle. Among the electronic gadgets in this house—television, CD player, personal computer with modem—the most daunting is the home alarm system. I'm supposed to disarm and then rearm it when I go out the door. Although I watched intently as this process of pushing buttons in complicated sequences was demonstrated the night before, I'm not so sure today that I can manage it without waking up my hostess, the neighbors, and whoever is on the other electronic end of the line at the local police station.

Whatever it is I do, however, it must be all right; the blinking lights on the box by the door stay green and no shrill beeping emerges from the speaker as I hurry out the door. There is my stick where I left it. Shaking the icy flecks of snow from it, I head off into the cold wind.

That alarm almost bested me, but high technology usually takes little skill to operate. That's one of its advantages, in fact: You don't have to know anything about it, and the device can autonomously work for you while you get on with your life. But when I consider my hostess back there, "safe" in her home because of her burglar alarm, I wonder if technology is really letting her get on with her life in the same way she would get on with it if the technology—in this case an alarm system—wasn't present.

We know many Friends and Amish who don't have

any keys to their homes. One mainstream Quaker couple leaves their second car, a Festiva, unlocked, parked on the curb of their village side street, with the ignition key in full view between the seats. Curt's explanation of this longtime habit is, "If somebody needs it that bad, they can have it."

Everyone on that street knows about the Festiva. They keep an eye on it, and it's never been stolen—only borrowed a few times.

To really be safe in our homes, don't we need the safety of other people? And even the safety of knowing that no matter what happens (because no alarm system can completely forestall thieves from breaking in, or keep moth and rust from corrupting our belongings), our ultimate protection is with God? Maybe the sophisticated alarm system lulls us, saps our awareness of the need for others and for the Lord's protection. Technology empowers, we are told, but who is empowered by it? To me it seems more and more to be something that puts us to sleep with regard to our true needs and their fulfillment.

In my earlier life, one of the things that began to wake me from my lack of awareness about how technology functions in our society was the question of who decided on the range of choices we have been given. Who made it hard to buy organic food at the supermarket but easy to buy food that had been factory-farmed? Who took away my neighbors and gave me a burglar alarm to replace them?

The biggest question for me today when it comes to the latest technology is this: Who is the ruler of the dream state of cyberspace?

The song that Mary Ann, Tasha, Jack, and Susanna

are singing this morning during their prayer time is "Morning Has Broken," a nice song for early spring, and a big hit for the former Cat Stevens. I can't do it justice stammering out the words between my clenched and chattering teeth. It's cold even with the ski mask over my face. It can't be more than fifteen degrees out—and that at the end of the second week in Fourth Month!

It was just this last Christmas that I think my question about the ruler of the dream state was answered, with a blasphemous image on a newsmagazine.

His name was JESUS ONLINE, but I didn't recognize him the first time I saw him: on the cover of *Time* magazine in December. Although the Internet's version of Jesus (who looks startlingly like traditional representations of Jesus Christ) gazed out at me from the magazine rack near the checkout counter at the Rite Aid—his name printed in large fluorescent letters across his chest: JESUS ONLINE—I barely noticed him.

I was feeling quite hemmed in by all the holiday shoppers, and something even stranger than the portrait on the cover of *Time* captured my attention. On the counter in front of the magazine rack stood a plastic model of a Victorian-era house. Little mechanical animals poked their heads out of its windows, digitally "singing" a Christmas carol in high, human-sounding cries. This rather monstrous toy was roaring out "Away in a Manger" (wah! WAAAH! wah! wah! WAH! WAH!) over and over.

The noise didn't seem to perturb anyone in the store but me. Even JESUS ONLINE, positioned on the magazine rack behind the toys, maintained his serene expression.

It was only when I saw the magazine again at the library a few days later that I registered the significance of *Time*'s cover image. The magazine had borrowed a representation of the face of Jesus Christ to illustrate "how the Internet is shaping our views of faith and religion." And, however unintentionally, they had given the Internet's god a name—JESUS ONLINE.

Electronic media, which fills the home of the woman who gave me a place to rest last night—television, computers, online networks—have transformed every area of our culture. So it shouldn't be surprising that the Internet would be developing its own version of religion. According to *Time*, the Internet is breeding new interest in every sort of religious experience and belief.

To the religious scholars and activists who log on, it must seem like a taste of heaven to find so many group discussions and resources. When I looked through *Time*'s profile, however, I found myself wondering: What is it about the medium that converts those who use it into believers in the Internet itself? *Time* quoted a number of Internet-using religious scholars who are now given to reciting enthusiastic heresies about how the Internet changes our very understanding of who God is. According to one (regrettably, a Hicksite Quaker professor of religion), "There is a shift to [the idea of] God as a process, evolving with us. If you believe in an eternal, unchanging God, you'll be in trouble."

You'll be in trouble?

With whom?

I think the professor was simply confused—like I was

for a minute in Rite Aid—and he mistook the Internet god for the real thing. But his quote could be taken for a prescient description of the Internet itself:

1. It's an omnipresent entity (like a "god").
2. It is changing its reality all the time.
3. If you don't align your reality with it,
   You'll be in trouble.

Certainly all the computer advertisements agree with number three when they intimate that your children risk some unimaginable penalty if you don't buy them a PC.

If you aren't part of the online world, this picture of the Internet as a mechanical divinity may seem far-fetched. Yet many who immerse themselves in the Internet use just such language in describing the medium's power. And the most influential voices in society—the electronic mouths of television that administer public discourse—keep repeating that the Internet is the technology of liberation, that it gives us godlike powers, and that the very nature of the network precludes centralization and control.

One time a social activist with a computer explained to me how she was using the powerful tools of the online world to resist oppression in the real world. But as she demonstrated, my eyes couldn't focus on the screen she was showing me. I watched her, sitting before the machine: her jaw slack yet her eyes alert; entranced, her mind removed and projected into another space that has its own power to change her merely by enveloping her—perhaps undermining the potency she believes the machine gives her.

Instead of liberation, what if the network itself presents a form of control? What if the limitations to normal thinking, sensing, *knowing* caused by the machine are redefining— I would say degrading—your humanity? Then cyberspace isn't necessarily just freeing you from the constraints of real life; it's actually molding you within its own terms. You have a new ruler, and it's a machine.

I ought to be more merciful toward the people who use the Internet—the beatitude I am trying to memorize today is *Blessed are the merciful: for they shall obtain mercy*—but I also need to note that mercifulness is not one of the character traits the online world seems to encourage. Among my acquaintances who use the World Wide Web on a regular basis, some have undergone a dramatic upshift in their emotional drive. Along with more forceful personalities (Cliff Stoll in his book *Silicon Snake Oil* calls them the "Ostrogoths and Visigoths of the Internet"), they have developed a peculiar reverence for the Internet experience itself. For them it is a world seemingly alive with the power of information. No wonder they are coming up with their own religion, as JESUS ONLINE so gnostically attested.

I've come back out on Route 40 and walked another three miles in the howling wind and snow. My destination today is Buckeye Lake, a fair distance up the road. Battling the wind has somehow gotten mixed up in my mind with battling the burglar alarm and the Internet. I feel a little crazy, in fact, as I reach the roadside town of Brownsville and slump onto a bench outside the closed-for-Sunday grocery store.

The snow has left off, but the cold wind remains, though I'm out of it at the moment here on my bench. Across the street sits the red-brick facade of the Coach House Inn, which has apparently closed up forever. It must have been built in the 1830s or 1840s as a tavern, and possibly a stagecoach stop along the National Road— probably just in time to enjoy a few years of heavy business prior to the collapse occasioned by the coming of first the Ohio and Erie Canal and then the railroads. Currently it's in desperate need of repair. The white Federalist-style home next to it is in fine shape, however.

I've only traveled five miles at most in the last hour and a half, but it seems much farther than that. Once I'm up and walking again, my pack starts to bother me under-neath the arm straps. To get my mind off of it, I decide to recite all the beatitudes I have memorized so far, hitching today's onto the end of each recitation:

Blessed are the merciful: for they shall obtain mercy.

I don't think the machine life many of us are living to-day is helping any when it comes to caring for others. I see myself as an innately selfish person, full of ego and self-will, and I really ought to avoid the dangers of alienation and merciless behavior I see being produced by modern life. So I go to what others might consider wild extremes to limit the extent to which modern technologies shape my own life.

I type on a Royal manual. In my work with *Plain* magazine I hand-feed the paper signatures into a hundred-year-old press. The wood engravings and hand-set type involve similarly personal, quiet technologies based on skill.

No hum of electricity pervades our home. We don't have a television, a computer, or even a radio. The tiny group of Christian Quakers to which I belong doesn't have a Web site. We have no way of keeping track of our Christian Peacemaker Team friends in other countries who communicate with stateside churches by e-mail. There is no modem, no printer, no online access to QuakeNet, the chat group set up by the Universalist-verging-on-pagan Quakers we split from long ago.

We are not in cyberspace. We are here, on the ground, in creation, all of the time.

This thought helps lighten my load: Even this cold wind is good, because it's real. I have to admit, however, that my pack is really bugging me now. I plan to unload some of the things in it after my next stop and ship them back home through the mail.

It's all uphill now, for about three miles, then all downhill for about two more. The black canvas straps of my pack feel like torture instruments as they rub against my sides. Finally I just have to stop beside the road and attempt to adjust them. Taking off the entire pack, I fiddle with the little metal braces that hold on the straps. Voilà! Much better.

Is there going to be anywhere to eat something today? There's no way to tell from the map hanging from my backpack. I'd originally planned to take today off from walking and find a Friends meeting to attend, but there aren't any along this leg of the journey. Anyhow, it seems appropriate to be out here walking on the Lord's Day. In fact, it seems worshipful.

Merely choosing to resist the Internet doesn't make us superior to those who embrace it. But I do think this choice makes Mary Ann and me more *like* the majority of people on this planet, who, after all, live without fax machines and e-mail accounts. By living more traditionally, we are discovering a different world of concerns and experiences than that of our more connected peers.

As my family has moved toward a more low-tech lifestyle, we have increasingly sensed the gift of the Holy Spirit becoming more substantially present in our lives. And this is a presence we are experiencing more intimately and more fully as we have become quieter. In the absence of the power of electronics, our brains have become more still. I would like to believe that we have also become more merciful and tender, like our Lord.

Today Mary Ann and the children are having meeting at home. Normally we would be on our way by now to the meetinghouse, courtesy of Ned the wonder horse, and soon would be settled in together on a bench in the silence of waiting worship. Silence! What a remarkable thing that it still exists at the end of the twentieth century, here in our little meetinghouse. Moreover, these people are gathered together in the silence for a purpose: to wait upon the Lord. Somewhere in the hour or so we are together, someone will probably be moved to rise and speak in the power of the Holy Spirit. That person is our neighbor—not a paid preacher, but a member of our community.

Some might charge that we are unfairly privileged because we have genuine community when many others in our country do not. I have heard it said by some Christians that virtual community is better than no community at all.

My experience here in "real" reality is that there's no substitute for genuine community, what the Amish call brotherhood. If community is what we lack, then that is what we must seek to create—not an ersatz version based on computer networks.

Real community functions not at all like a network, which is made to exchange information and other cultural goods among many points or "nodes." Real community—that is, a community of people sharing one another's real-life burdens and joys—is not to be found in the exchange of anything that merely connects us, be it information or labor or material goods. In community we are *giving*, not exchanging. Here in person, we share ourselves, finding our love for one another in God's great, merciful love of us.

Wendell Berry says that the difference between the advice of an agricultural economist and that of a neighbor is that the economist isn't around when your crop fails. I would apply this maxim to the difference between online and real communities. The loving accountability essential to true community isn't something that can be grafted onto unreal cyberspace. Those who use the Internet to forge communities to do good in the world may be changed for the worse by their interface with a machine existence that is lacking in these necessary qualities.

When my (real) community gathers for worship to transact our business (which we do corporately, in "meeting for worship with attention to business") we may meet in one another's homes, as the Amish do, or in a meetinghouse, but never in a "church," because we recognize the church as the body of believers rather than the building where they meet. Our attachment to place for our community has to do with our physical gathering, rather than a particular location. We can meet anywhere, as Mary Ann and the children are proving today in the silence of our living room. Our Christian worship is fully portable, but it isn't *virtual*. It is solidly real. I'm reminded of what the Spirit sings in Psalm 127: "Except the Lord build the house, they labor in vain that build it."

The Lord's house is built low, close to the ground. It's a stable, a tomb carved from the rock. It is in us—each one of us—right here in the real world. My walk today can be that house, no matter how hard the wind blows.

At the crossroad of Jacksontown there is a gas station and a restaurant, Clark's. After a quick meal there I feel ready for the last leg of today's trip. There's still a long way to go on Route 40, after which I'll turn off to the south and head for a campground near Buckeye Lake.

Traffic has thinned out now that most churchgoers are back home. The highway that parallels my road to Columbus, Interstate 70, is almost empty of cars and trucks when I pass under it at the Buckeye Lake interchange. Beyond the ring of fast-food outlets and gasoline pit stops south of the interstate, I happen to notice a sign for my campground, with an arrow pointing me in the direction I'm headed and the fact that it is still one and a half miles ahead. Back home that would be the distance from my door to the local grocery store.

The sun is out of the clouds occasionally now and it's maybe a little warmer, though it feels quite cold yet. Buckeye Lake is a summer tourist town crammed with little one- and two-room houses and small bungalows; obviously these were originally intended as summer homes. Now most of them appear to be occupied year-round by an impoverished working-class population.

But where do they work? It must be that many commute to Columbus, which is less than thirty-five miles from here.

I haven't caught sight of the lake yet, though I mistook a huge white storage building for it when I saw it far ahead where the road must curve off to the west again. I wend my way along the sidewalk, stepping around motorboats parked in the drives of little stick houses. The boats are covered on their decks and inside with brightly colored indoor-outdoor carpeting.

The snow and the overcast sky have done nothing to raise my spirits. I'm even wondering if there actually is a lake at all. Buckeye Lake was originally dammed to make a reservoir for the Ohio Canal—maybe they've drained it again to make way for all this expanse of overbuilt, touristy vacation living. I can hear myself complaining—ugh. But

I don't see that lake—not once, all the way to the campground, past the drive-through bait shops and the "Ammo/ Camo" store.

All my grousing, though, falls silent when I reach the camp. It's a strange thing to walk into a three- or four-acre campsite that doesn't have more than a couple of trees. Instead, there are six long rows of parking spaces, the last of which—number 205—butts up against a short row of four cabins. But they aren't even real cabins. There's a sign pointing to them that declares they are "Kabins," and so they are: mass-produced storage sheds on skids, the kind you see for sale out in front of big hardware stores. The kind that a lot of Amish guys bang together in their home shops with an air-powered nail gun and raw wood. And one of them is mine.

I'm whining and feeling sorry for myself. These shelters look more like rude doghouses than the little log cabins in the woods I imagined when I planned my pilgrimage. Each Kabin has a couple of windows cut into it and a miniature picnic table out front. Maybe they call it a "pik-nik" table.

Slowly turning about in a circle, I can't imagine what it is like here in the summer, or who would want to spend their vacation existence in the company of eight hundred other people on a treeless parking lot. And why am I here, in this sad place eighty-five miles from home?

I'm too cold to hold on to my big display of self-pity. I rush into the manager's-office-cum-store, where I have a long but nicely warming wait while the two clerks on duty do major battle with their computer to find my reservation.

A quick inspection trip shows that there isn't a chair in my Kabin, just a bunk made out of two-by-fours and plywood with a foam pad, so I borrow a chair from the laundry room. There also are no sheets, pillows, or blankets. Okay. I run across the road to the Krazy Kat Dollar Store and buy what I need. I didn't want to lug my sleeping bag on this walk, and now I'm paying for it.

Actually, this Kabin isn't so bad. I would have preferred more spartan accommodations along the route than I've had up till now, because that is more in keeping with my daytime pilgrimage. I'm starting to think of this journey more expressly as a pilgrimage; I veered away from calling it that to myself until lately because I couldn't figure out what it was a pilgrimage *to*. The Ohio Bureau of Motor Vehicles? Idly I pull the driver's license from my coat pocket. That would be ridiculous. Maybe that's not my real and final destination on this trip, and I just have to have faith it's a pilgrimage to somewhere a little more worthy.

Setting the license on the bunk, I get up for a moment to drape my coat over the uncurtained window, where the evening sun is streaming in. On second thought, I take it back away; the sunlight might help warm the room.

This trip has on occasion struck others as silly, too. A week ago a dozen of us were sitting around a table in the kitchen of Stillwater meetinghouse after an evening prayer meeting, the twilight flooding the ancient wavy panes of glass above us.

The conversation had turned to the coming week and our individual plans. This seemed like a good time to mention that I planned to walk to Columbus (I had already discussed my plan with a few discerning elders).

"You're what?" several people said at the same time.

"I'm walking from Barnesville to Columbus next week. It's about a hundred and twenty miles. I'm going there to return my driver's license to the Bureau of Motor Vehicles," I added, trying to be helpful. That wasn't the only reason I was going, of course, but it was the only one that was easy to put into words.

Down at the other end of the table Fred and Jean were shaking their heads and laughing. "But there's a BMV office half a mile from here at East End Garage!"

Boy, what would that crazy Scott do next?

Everyone was staring at me, so I told them about planning to give up my car-driving privileges for good. I talked about my changing perceptions about the automobile age as I learned to drive a horse and buggy, and how not having a license would mean I could never participate in car culture, would in fact mostly be limited to traveling within a dozen-mile radius of home. So I wanted to walk to Columbus to see if I was really ready to make that sacrifice.

One of the things I couldn't yet articulate to the prayer group was that I wanted to get rid of the license itself. Since then I've been considering both the benefits and problems of my driver's license, and I've seen that part of my need to let it go has to do with its threat to my privacy. The little piece of laminated cardboard I'm flipping over and over on the bunk mattress has achieved a certain kind of mastery over me that I want to be freed from.

Over the years, I have developed an increasingly "unofficial" life. I've become a virtual unknown in the record books of The Powers That Be. Our whole family has pretty much disappeared, sliding free of the entanglements of bureaucracy, consumerism, and the omnipresent data banks. My driver's license is something of a sticking point in this regard. Holding on to it has continued to make me known to those who, to be honest about it, really don't know or care about me at all.

The license presents an admirably concentrated representation of a general problem: Its power is to grant me a privilege in exchange for collecting the facts of my life into an official portrait. This portrait has the effect of reducing me to a collection of naked facts, the better to successfully channel my (in this case driving) behavior.

The thought that one is controlled by unseen forces—even the Bureau of Motor Vehicles—is often a perception of the deluded, I know. Let me qualify my paranoia by affirming that all the unseen forces gathering my personal data probably have no actual interest in me, nor any enmity toward me. "They," after all, are keeping the same data on you, too, and just about everyone else. The truly paranoid person lives with the constant self-aggrandizing delusion that the hostile forces that control him have an obsessive interest in him. My experience, on the other hand, and probably yours as well, is quite the opposite of this.

What is instead most overpowering about the invasion of our identities is its routine, impersonal nature. If anything, the constant demand for quantification of ourselves, and the unending uses of us this allows, teaches us again and again that we do not matter as people.

And so, in the case of my driver's license, anything that facilitates the regulation and "use" of me as a driver is known. But none of what is known of my identity (and I would rather have kept much of it private) holds any personal or human interest to those who know it.

Holding the license still for a moment, I catalog its seen and unseen descriptors: My photograph. My Social Security number. My age. The height, weight, and color of my body. The description of my hair and eyes. My physical limitations. My dwelling place. And, indirectly by way of files linked to my license number, my driving record (fair: two speeding tickets, two minor accident citations, and a warning in twenty-two years), my insurance coverage, my bank account. From any of these it is a relatively simple matter to discover other public and private details of my life on paper or in computer databases. Furthermore, in the brief space of time between when I last renewed my license and when it is set to expire, the driving privilege has been computerized. A digital photograph and holographic image hover on the new licenses, along with an identity bar code and a data strip capable of holding an additional five- or six-page dossier. In brief, the technology alone is leading in the opposite direction from where I want to go.

Putting my older, nondigital license in a zippered pouch on the outside of my pack, I hop up and make an effort to make the Kabin a little more tidy and snug. The plastic bag the blanket came in gets ripped into two pieces, which I stuff into the large ventilation grilles at each end of the room under the roof beam. Now the wind isn't blowing through the inside anymore. After taking out the Bible and rearranging the rest of the pack's contents, I use the pack itself as a canvas pillow.

After prayers for my family, for my safety, and for the woman living alone who gave me shelter last night, the room seems to have warmed somewhat. It may be that the last rays of sun making it in through the little window have done their job.

It's not seven o'clock yet, but I lie down in my coat and sweatshirt underneath the blanket. Opening the Bible to the very beginning, I turn on my side to read, and instead fall instantly and soundly asleep.

The Sixth Day

Blessed are the pure of heart: for they shall see God.

It's not as cold this morning in my Kabin as I would have thought. Even though I had to get up in the night and stumble through the dark to the outdoor rest room, I feel like I got a good night's sleep.

Today is the one-year anniversary of my speech to the delegates at the Second Luddite Congress. It's also the sixth day of my pilgrimage, although I don't intend to go very far today. The first chapter of Genesis says that on the fifth day of creation God made all the life of the sea and of the air, and on the sixth day He made all the life on the land:

> And God made the beast of the earth after his kind,
> and the cattle after their kind, and every thing
> that creepeth upon the earth after his kind:
> And God saw that it was good.

As a Christian who loves being in nature, I find these to be important words. On the sixth day God goes on to create humans—but even before He does, He has already pronounced the living world as pleasing *to Him*. It's His, and He's glad He made it.

Environmentalists, many of whom are fervently anti-Christian, prefer to note the next verse, in which God gives us "dominion over the fish of the sea, and over the fowl of the air, and over the cattle, and over all the earth, and over every creeping thing that creepeth upon the earth," as proof our religion is bent on destroying nature.

Well, it can't be gainsaid. Call it what you will—stewardship, domination, whatever—it certainly isn't a command to celebrate "wild Nature" as the highest being in the universe. Yet I think that my life today, so much of which revolves around tending the gardens around my house and caring for the horse and goats we have dominion over, actually makes me much more able to appreciate wildness—as *good*. As God's handiwork.

Before I left my job as an administrative bureaucrat, I always wanted to spend time out in nature. It was exasperating to have the day begin and end with my body stuffed into a car for the commute to and from work. When I could plan time to spend out-of-doors, however, I often felt dissatisfied with the experience. It was as if I still could not break through to nature, even in the middle of a wooded park or at the edge of the sea. Spending most of my time in artificial environments just made it even harder to let the nonhuman world of creation soak into me during those few times I could get away.

Now that I'm more frequently engaged in the natural world—as I "dominate" it to grow our own food and keep our transportation unit (Ned) alive—I feel much closer to it. And I love nature for its own sake, not just for what it can do for me. That would make me a deep ecologist, I guess, except for one thing: I'm a Christian, an importer of hegemony and patriarchy, and I refuse to agree that humans are no different from the rest of the things "that creepeth upon the earth."

As a child, I spent a great deal of time in nature, wandering through a second-growth maple-birch woodland in the formerly glaciated northwestern edge of the Allegheny Plateau. I was never accompanied on my outings by anyone who knew either those facts or the names and attributes of the living things of that place. I grew up botanically and zoologically illiterate.

Nowadays I find that I have learned a lot about nature, especially plants, just by studying my homestead and what is historically native to it. *Woody Plants of Ohio*, by Lucy E. Braun, often gets shoved into my wide inner coat pocket before one of my daily walks. That leaves my hands free to grasp the outstretched hands of children who want to walk with me and learn the names and ways of natural life.

This winter, while plotting my trip to Columbus on the map, I was excited to find that the route would take me close to Buckeye Lake. I knew I had to stop here and see the floating bog called Cranberry Island—that incredible remnant of a lost wilderness that once dwelt all along the edge of the glaciers. Cranberry Island is also interesting as an artifact of Ohio transportation, its status akin to that of old, abandoned stagecoach inns on the side of the National Road. Only in this case, the primary cause of the island was not a road, but rather the Ohio Canal.

In 1830 a 4,300-acre reservoir was made here. Its purpose was to provide the canal locks with the water necessary to lift passenger boats and freight barges over the divide between the Scioto and Licking River basins. As the waters of the "Big Swamp"—actually a huge ice-age wetland—rose behind the dam, the entire valley was inundated and destroyed. All, that is, except the most recently growing (and therefore most buoyant) section of the swamp's huge peat bog, which floated to the surface of the new lake.

The floating island came into existence because of the strange and unique ability of sphagnum (peat) moss to absorb lots and lots of water. The plant has an unusual structure that features large, empty cells that take in water and small, flat chlorophyll cells packed in between. Even after these large cells die, they can still absorb water. They make the typical peat bog a thick, spongy mat of saturated plant material. Those cells that are not full of water are full of air, making the mat quite able to float in the water.

What helps the mats of moss become so large, even after most of the underlying plant material has died, is that the dead parts don't decay. And that is because the living parts of sphagnum moss release acid into the surrounding water—lots of acid. Huge mats create very acid conditions, which preserve the dead portions.

Because of the buoyancy of this huge peat "swamp," an area of about fifty acres "stretched and expanded like a waterlogged sponge" (as the park information guide puts it) when the lake was flooded. The heart of the cranberry bog was lifted up and out from underneath the waters to become an island.

This morning I need to check at the campground office to see if my permit to go onto the island has arrived in the mail. I applied several months ago to the state's Division of Natural Areas and Preserves, but the stamped permit arrived at my home two days after I left for Columbus. Mary Ann has mailed it here to the campground. It wasn't yet on hand last night, but it came in this morning's mail.

Opening it, I see that the office has returned my original application form (under "The intended purpose of your visit is:" I wrote, "I am traveling a portion of the National Road on foot and writing about technology and nature. I will spend a day at the bog to experience this unique occurrence"). Along with a yellow permit slip and a map is this note:

> At present, we cannot provide boat transportation to the island except for guided group tours, and the local marina is no longer in operation. Assuming you can arrange boat transportation, be sure to dock at one of the two docks on the north side and stay on the boardwalk during your visit.

Well, I have a permit, but no way to get onto the island. Calling the local state park office yields the name of a lakeside restaurant where I might be able to get someone to help me. Since I'm coming back to my Kabin to spend another night, I don't take much with me—just a snack, a pad of paper, and a few other small items that fit in my coat pockets.

It's a beautiful, sunny day, already much warmer than yesterday. I need to retrace my steps as far as the interstate, which I do with some pain. I didn't realize until now how much yesterday's long, cold walk tired my body. I have to walk east and then south on Hunt's Landing Road until I get to the end, where the Blue Goose Restaurant sits by the water.

After some introductions and negotiations with the owner, a young man with a broken arm and a black eye ("I'm the bouncer here on weekends," he tells me) starts the engine on a small boat and steers us (with one arm) a ways up the lake to the north side of Cranberry Island. His engine cuts out just then, and while he tries to restart it with his good arm pulling the cord, I wander up the landing, a little confused as to whether this is really a cranberry bog at all. In front of the dock is a thicket of trees on both sides of a boardwalk of wide wooden planks.

But as I walk further in, I see that past this initial clump of trees there are two or three acres of low, rolling hummocks—one- to two-foot swells capped by squat shrubs. Back behind me the motor kicks in and the boat heads back to shore.

These shrubs, a few inches high and sprawling every which way, are cranberry plants—in this case *Vaccinium macrocarpon*, or large cranberry. They form a low-growing mat of stems and small leaves. The rounded tip of the leaves is my only clue that these are the large variety of berries, which grow in somewhat less acidic conditions than the small cranberry plant.

It's not possible to tell where one plant leaves off and another begins; they weave through and tumble over the humps of peat moss. Cranberry shrubs clone new plants off their stems as they are covered and rooted in the moss.

I had expected that there would still be some cranberries clinging to these plants, as they tend to hold on to their berries over the winter. The berries are a welcome snack for overflying birds in the early spring return migration. But these plants appear to have already been picked clean.

The tangle of brownish stems and evergreen leaves hides the profusion of roots that are wadded into the sphagnum moss "hump" below. Down in the mat the temperature stays much cooler than soil on land, so growing seasons for many of the bog plants are also much shorter, more like the summers in Canada, where these plants originated. Even this early in the year, however, the cranberry hillocks have a soft beauty; "decent weeds, at least, which widowed Nature wears," as Thoreau said of his New England marshes at winter's end. This beauty is enhanced by the well-worn look of the surrounding plants in this relatively diverse bog community; the sedges in particular almost glow with an inner light. These dead clumps of paper-thin herbs—similar to grasses—grow around and between the upwelling cranberry hummocks.

In fact, the abundance of sedge plants (genus *Carex*) tells me the acidity of the peat mat may be less than in a normal peat bog. Some species of sedge thrive in bogs, but they are usually transitional from a less acidic fen to a more acidic bog. Here the process may be reversing itself. The bog's acidity probably *is* declining. That is another reason I wanted to come here today to see the island, because from all reports it is doomed.

In the 169 years since it popped back up out of Buckeye Lake, the island has shrunk from its original fifty acres down to a last-reported total of nineteen. On the way over here today the bouncer told me that another ten or more acres sank during a bad storm on the lake a few years back. Looking from my limited vantage point on the boardwalk, I estimate that only eight or nine acres remain. This bog is inherently unstable: Whereas every other peat bog grows out from land into water, this one is instead surrounded by water, making it more likely that parts will break off from wave action and the wake of passing motorboats.

Even in the most open part of the bog that I can see today, there are little invading alder saplings. The trees that have taken root on the island further destabilize it when they eventually die and fall over, pulling up big sections of the peat along with their own root systems.

Walking to another part of the island, I find myself in a grove of full-size maple trees. The ground on either side of the boardwalk is still squishy peat, but there's a small pond over which the walk passes that looks like it could be in any hardwood forest setting, instead of on a floating bog island. While I was waiting for the bouncer to bring me here, I looked at some photographs of the lake tacked to the walls of the Blue Goose. Several shots taken from an airplane over the lake show no trees at all on this island. The photos are all from the 1920s.

In the watery leaf litter next to the boardwalk is what looks like wild calla. I'm not sure, because it also looks a lot like jack-in-the-pulpit at this stage, a plant I'm much more familiar with. These three hooded stems stand just a few inches high, each with a curved-over, rather ruffle-edged cowl made of a single whitish leaf. Soon these leaves will lift up to reveal a stubby flower spike with pretty—but smelly—yellow florets.

The thought of that suddenly makes me realize that the weird green shoots I saw jutting up from a muddy patch of sedge not far from here are probably skunk cabbage, with their spathes (the leaf covering the flower) that look like rolled-up newspapers. Skunk cabbage plants, like some sedges, are bog associates, but they, too, favor less acidic conditions, which may be occurring here in the more compromised environs of the island.

Three red-winged blackbirds sweep down into an alder tree. One male is hopping about, *chip-chip*ping at me. In his view I'm clearly out of place here on his island.

At the end of the boardwalk is another dock, from which I can see the shore and the crush of houses at its edge. A screen door bangs, a dog gives a short, muffled yap—the island is so close to this part of the north shore of the lake I could have swum out here.

How is it, I wonder, for birds and other animals to find their places shrinking and disappearing? I think of them looking for the physical cues that prompt their natural behaviors, only to be confused by what has taken nature's place—and smacking into the mirrored windows of office buildings. My favorite nature writer, the Amish farmer

David Kline, ended an essay about endangered species of birds with the same verses from the Book of Genesis I read this morning:

> But overall our record is nothing to be proud of. God gave man "dominion over the fish of the sea, and over the fowls of the air, and over the cattle and over all the earth, and over every creeping thing that creepeth upon the earth." Are we to be wise stewards, or does this give us the right to exploit, abuse, and exterminate His creation?

A large speedboat lumbers by on the water, going slowly through the posted no-wake zone around the island. Another reason to give up my driver's license is to become more firmly wedded to the place where I live, so that my stewardship yields some protection for the natural life around me. Part of Wendell Berry's "Work Song" comes to me: "I work to renew a ruined place / that no life be hostage of my comfort."

I have been here for four or five hours now. It's very tranquil, although the island is so close to the shore that I can hear people beginning to prepare evening meals in their kitchens. The blue of the sky is as soft as the muted browns and purples of the bog. The redwings have settled into sweet burbles of singing. I realize now that this place is a sanctuary, not only a threatened bit of Canadian flora but a connected part of a living and changing whole. How could anyone who reads Scripture believe the roots of Judeo-Christian belief are antinature? God puts us in His stead, but He also confirms His own love and relationship with His world. He tells Noah and his sons that all life is delivered into their hands, yes, but then He makes his covenant not to destroy the world again not only with humans, but with "every living creature" and "every beast of the earth." In the last book of the New Testament, Saint John the Divine describes all of creation worshiping the Lamb of God:

> And every creature which is in heaven, and on the earth, and under the earth, and such as are in the sea, and all that are in them, I heard saying, Blessing, and honor, and glory, and power, be unto Him that sitteth upon the throne, and unto the Lamb for ever and ever.

So tell me: What would happen if we caused one of these creatures to cease to exist, or otherwise interfered with the creation's ability to worship its Creator? Christians obviously have a strong duty to uphold God's care for His creatures, with whom He has a relationship independent of us.

I am finding it difficult to know, however, what exactly could be done in the case of Cranberry Island. Neither the new nature of hardwood thicket nor the old nature of the bog will be here shortly. This place is doomed. And it should also be noted that the original, unflooded bog that was here before Buckeye Lake was also quite probably in flux; it existed as a remnant of an ecosystem that disappeared from this area thousands of years ago. Part of God's creation is its attribute of ceaseless change.

Three happy-sounding Canada geese cruise by overhead on their way to somewhere else. Early evening is a good time to see some of the water birds moving about. A blue heron makes a slow glide along the shoreline across from me, then over to the bog and past some trees to where she is out of view. Cranberries got their name from the blue heron, which was called a crane by New England settlers—hence crane-berries.

It is getting late in the day, the shadows of the trees stretching across the hummocks of the bog. I stoop down for a while to examine some bug-eating pitcher plants that are common in colonies here, and then head back to the little pool underneath the boardwalk. In this spot, below the maples, I can see the cranberry hillocks, where a number of American sparrows seem to be having a game of some sort in the sedge clumps. It could be hide-and-seek, or they could be feeding on last year's seeds among the plants. One flies away into the half moon right above us in the blue, blue sky.

The air down close to the ground is now noticeably warmer than that higher up. The bog provides some climate control with its thermal mass of waterlogged peat, making it a nice place for ducks to nest. I can hear some quacking over by the shore. The pool around me has leaves floating in it and some green algae, but no fish or other visible critters. Sitting in the quiet, I find myself slipping into the posture of waiting worship, as if I were in Friends meeting at home.

Is this quiet feeling a form of nature worship, then?

No, but I've been reading in the book of nature today, and it's pointed me back to the Source. How could I ever have thought that all that is good in nature—and so much is marvelous and wonderful—has no author? The environmentalists often are hostile to Christianity (and to individual Christians, too) because they believe Christianity begat Western civilization, and Western civilization is anti-nature. But how to explain the Anabaptists, the Friends, and other Christian denominations that acknowledge our responsibility to the garden? How to explain this verse:

"The earth is the Lord's; and the fullness thereof."

Of course, there are many environmentalists, especially those who practice "deep ecology," who understand our faithfulness to the God of creation.

It has been, I suppose, a half hour or so now that I've been sitting here fairly motionless. Now a male mallard duck has just waddled over from somewhere to my left; he's combing through some clumps of sedge with his beak and poking around in the leaf litter. It is restful just to watch him idling along. Finally he drops into the pool near me and quietly drifts around for a few minutes. I doubt there's anything edible in this water. He hasn't noticed me. When he paddles off the other way I quietly get up and walk back down to the dock to wait for my return ride to shore. The sun is going down, and more birds are visiting the island. A jay and a robin both alight in the tree overhanging the dock. I worry for a moment that no one will come for me, but that thought slides away. Something good has happened to me here—I'm calm. All the tensions and doubts about my trip that I experienced yesterday seem to have been relieved for now.

My water taxi arrives at about six o'clock. On shore a twenty-dollar bill completes the transaction, and I'm free to walk back to my Kabin, three miles away. I don't think it will be as cold tonight. Tomorrow I want to leave early and get to my next stop before noon, so that I can catch up on my journal and get ready for the following day's walk into Columbus.

A Day of Rest

*Blessed are the peacemakers: for they shall be
called the children of God.*

The only place to write in my motel room is on top of the
little plastic end table next to the bed. It's one o'clock in
the afternoon, and I'm already at Reynoldsburg, my final
stop before Columbus. I intend to take it easy today, resting my body and catching up in my journal. I don't mind
having to use this little table to write on—I'm just so happy
that I've made it this far. Today's song from my household's morning devotions is "Teach Me Kingdom Ways,"
and I'm belting it out now in my little room, adding a
little syncopation and bluesy inflection. When I do that at
home, everyone simultaneously covers their ears and rolls
their eyes.

The journey this morning was uneventful, as smooth
and level as the terrain in these parts has become. I started
out on a country road south of Route 40 that runs parallel
to it, setting out into the cold starlight at five-thirty. Pulling
my ski mask over my face, I fairly ran the first three miles.
The newspaper I read at the truck stop where I paused for

coffee was the only one I had looked at in a week. One article on the front page caught my eye: "Bank Robber at Large," detailing a robbery the previous day in the town of Newark, just north of there. According to the story, the robber was still on the loose, last seen on foot headed south toward . . . Route 40 and the interstate. Witnesses at the crime scene described him as having a pale complexion; about my height and build, wearing a black coat and a black ski mask.

My ski mask happens to be dark gray, not black, but I elected nevertheless not to put it back on. Instead, out came the trusty broad-brimmed hat. Surely no robber would wear such a hat.

My body felt especially good this morning, after yesterday's briefer walks to and from the Blue Goose and a good night's rest. I was able to continue my brisk pace across the flat landscape and made excellent time, only stopping briefly at a post office to cram some of the unneeded items from my backpack into a Priority Mail carton to send home. At ten-thirty I halted at the eastern edge of Reynoldsburg and took this room for the night, having come about fourteen miles.

Paging through the little memo book of notes I took while on Cranberry Island, I can't help but think of yesterday's experience as an allegory: the bog that wouldn't allow itself to be flooded out of existence as a symbolic retelling of the history of the plain people and their resistance to modernity. According to the reasoning of the Industrial Age, neither the plain people nor the cranberry bog should exist in the current reality. Yet here is the bog, a living time traveler from another, premodern ecosystem; and here are the Amish, the Old Order Mennonites, the Hutterites and German Brethren, the River Brethren, and some remnant of the Wilburite "plain" Friends, a spectral range of living alternatives to an otherwise all-encompassing modernity.

The bog's presence reminds us that we can't always make nature do what we want it to. The Amish and other plain people remind us that modernity can't always make people do what it wants them to. Plain living, in fact, with its sincerity, its simple pleasures, and its independent security, gives the lie to modern life's most central piece of propaganda, which is that the mechanistic utopia of the consumer society has made people happier, safer, and more powerful than in the "bad old days" before microwave ovens and color TV.

How unfortunate for modernity that a piece of the "bad old days" has refused to be drowned, has been preserved and now floats on the lake of culture at the end of the twentieth century. A living, functioning part of our history is available for comparison with the wonders of modern life. As we look at the two cultures side by side—the one agrarian, religious, slow-paced, morally strict, and technologically small-scale, the other industrial and bureaucratic, materialistic, frantically paced, morally confused, and technologically advanced to the point of exceeding any and every physical limit previously known to mankind—we see that no positive claim about modernity need go unchallenged. We have an alternative model, alive, up and running, with which to compare it.

Nothing more is going to happen today on my pilgrimage, other than writing down events in my journal. The bedspread has been thrown over the television set, so there isn't any easy escape into virtual reality. This is probably a good moment in which to step away from the journey to Columbus and try to explain to you—and possibly to myself—one of the reasons, at least, why I am making it. The only way I can truly explain is to tell you a story, one I told to the delegates of the Second Luddite Congress a year ago yesterday.

Once upon a time, near the place where I grew up, there was a Swiss cheese factory. Every year the elementary school I attended took field trips to this cheese factory (my oldest sister threw up in the middle of her tour due to the sights and smells), and the factory was known far and wide for its outstanding product.

The "cheese house," as it was called locally, was owned as a cooperative. Three hundred Amish farmers, all from the same community, formed the cooperative in the 1950s in order to solve a problem they had encountered: new federal regulations that required milk consumed in liquid form to be refrigerated from the moment it left the cow. The only way to meet this new requirement for grade-A milk would be to install electrically run bulk cooling tanks. But the Amish did not have electricity.

The dairy farmers didn't protest or try to change the government's rules. Instead they formed the cooperative so they would have a place to send their grade-B unrefrigerated milk and have it made into cheese. (The Amish milked their cows by hand, collected the milk in pails, and stored it in ten-gallon cans set in cold-water troughs until the milk truck picked it up.)

A master cheese maker from Switzerland was hired by the co-op, and the ownership of the business was split between the farmers, who owned the buildings and the land, and the cheese maker, who, because he was not Amish, could own and operate the modern electric equipment used to make the cheese. In this way, the Amish were assured of a continuing market for their low-tech milk but did not get involved in modern production.

The business prospered. Soon the brand name of the factory's Swiss cheese was known throughout the region, and production increased every year. As the business grew, other suppliers of milk had to be added to augment the output of the Amish dairy farmers. By the end of the 1980s the cheese maker found that almost 90 percent of the milk needed to make his cheese was coming from outside the Amish community, from big farms with bulk cooling tanks. It took a lot less work to test and process this grade-A milk that was coming in on huge refrigerated tanker trucks than it did to deal with lower-grade milk delivered in beat-up ten-gallon cans.

Then the cheese maker, who had somewhere along the way been made the company owner, dropped dead of a heart attack.

The cheese maker's son, who had spent much of his life so far working for the company, became the new president. Soon after his father's death, he called together the membership of the cooperative to make an announcement: Either the Amish would agree to convert their farms to handle grade-A milk, or he would no longer accept their grade-B milk and they would have to sell their shares to him. An ultimatum, just as simple as that. Modernize, or be ruined.

Now, I had kept in touch with this story mostly from accounts in the local papers, because I was living about forty miles away at the time of the factory president's announcement. But I knew some of the farms that would be affected, and I knew how strongly the Amish leadership wanted to keep the modernizing influence of electricity out of their communities. (Imagine, if you can, a twenty-square-mile area of beautiful nature and farmland *with not a single telephone pole or electric line*.) Not only would electricity for bulk cooling tanks lead to the temptation for other higher-tech farming equipment, but the tanks themselves would make it possible for the first time to produce and temporarily store more milk than a family could produce by hand milking. That could lead to more cows, hired help, larger fields to produce more feed, and the larger, more modern equipment needed for working more land. Not to mention more milking equipment and a bigger milk check—which meant more spending on more "necessities." In short, the addition of bulk tanks, now as in the 1950s, would lead to the cycle of boom and bust that had already wiped out many of the non-Amish smallholders in the 1980s.

The alternative, however, was even more difficult to contemplate. Without a market for their milk—the cheese maker's son had given them a one-year period before he would bar their milk from the factory—three hundred dairy farms would be out of business. These farms were mostly clustered together in the very heart of the Amish community; they provided its cash wealth and were its conservative anchor against the changes in the larger society that were eating away at the edges of plain life.

The cheese maker's son had them over a barrel, and he knew it. They would have to give in. They could still be true to their religious beliefs, he said, by using gasoline-fueled generators to power their refrigerated tanks. "We'd love to take their grade-A milk," the paper quoted him, "and we'll pay them a great price."

My own response back in those days was to urge them to resist. I remember telling my bride of less than a year that we ought to *help them!* We could write letters of protest to the editor of the paper, decrying the actions of the cheese maker's son and demanding legal action. After all, it wasn't right and it wasn't fair (I had a keen sense of justice back then). We were both recently retired environmental activists who knew how to raise a ruckus: We could picket the cheese factory! (No doubt we would be chanting that peculiarly powerless generic cry we'd been taught to holler while marching past the White House on other protest occasions:

WHAT DO WE WANT?
GRADE-B MILK!
WHEN DO WE WANT IT?
NOW!)

But the Amish never considered either of the possibilities. They didn't resist and they didn't give in. They just asked for their shares—worth about two thousand dollars per farmer—and they walked away.

Then they built a new cheese house.

They built it on their own, adding to their monetary shares in the project all the energy and time that otherwise would have gone either into litigation to fight back or into complying with the milk regulations that went against their principles. That time and work helped make up for the setback of having to abandon their co-op and start from scratch.

This time they *did* get a lawyer before hiring their next cheese maker—"not to fight," as one farmer said, "but to understand." So that the same thing wouldn't happen again.

But that isn't the end of the story. In their Anabaptist Christian wisdom, the Amish dairy farmers didn't just leave their old factory and its owner with anger and bitterness. On the contrary: As a courtesy to the cheese maker's son, the new cheese cooperative promised that at first it would make only colby, Monterey Jack, muenster—but not Swiss cheese. That would keep them from taking away any of his business.

Why would they do that? To be nice? To "repay good for evil," as Jesus instructs? To be peacemakers?

No Amishman would do what I am doing, traveling on foot to the seat of power to give back a privilege, yet I believe that through my more Quakerly method of witnessing, I am emulating the Amish ethic of nonresistance.

I'm willing to go the extra mile—several, in fact—beyond either resisting or complying. I'm coming to Columbus to cash in my share of modernity, and then I'm heading back home, where a few hundred thousand plain Christians are building a kingdom based on the plan of a different architect—a Master Builder.

If we had a motto, it might be the opposite of the one I heard in the 1960s telling us to "turn on, tune in, and drop out." Our revolutionary slogan could urge the world to turn off (virtual reality), tune out (advertising and materialism), and drop in (on your neighbors, to let them know it's time to stop being lonely in America). Drop in—into something more real, more loving, than what you're currently experiencing.

A revolution of hearts is being led by example, by the Amish, who mostly don't even know they *are* leading it. (That is, by the way, one common criticism of the Amish made by other Christians: Why don't they go out and evangelize more? The Amish seem content, though, to let their lives speak for them.)

During the Second Luddite Congress the Amish writer and farmer David Kline did confide his own understanding of community, of how broad it can be, encompassing all of creation. He described his earliest glimpse of community when, as a twelve-year-old boy, a government technician visited his father's farm. He came to measure the fields for compliance with government restrictions on wheat production, and he unrolled a large aerial photograph of the entire neighborhood onto the hood of his car:

I looked at the map and marveled at the landscape from the air—the view the red-tailed hawk had when it soared high over the fields. There, meandering through the pasturefield, was the creek where we fished and skinny-dipped. And the woods with all its interesting creatures. There was the one-room schoolhouse with its massive white oak by the front entrance and red oak next to the baseball backstop.

What David had spent his life learning—that community exists in the relationship between creation and Creator—was passed on to the delegates as free wisdom. Really, it is that wisdom of seeing our connectedness that led me to experience a vision of what it would be like if I gave up driving cars forever, period. That vision came to me exactly one year ago, today, on the final morning of the opening sessions of the Second Luddite Congress.

That day, the mighty Friends meetinghouse was packed with almost four hundred people, delegates from practically every state sitting in varying degrees of discomfort on the spartan Quaker benches. The building had a high ceiling, unadorned walls, absolutely plain woodwork—no microphones or public address system.

We had spent two days just listening to people: plain Christians such as David Kline; ecologists such as Bill McKibben and Stephanie Mills; farmers, including Art Gish and Gene Logsdon; a chronicler of technological folly, Bill Henderson; and a historian of technological resistance,

Kirk Sale. A brave traditional midwife spoke about the beauty of home birth and the draining, constant fight to save it from the government war on midwifery. John Taylor Gatto tried to trace the patterns that could explain how government schooling could have gone so wrong. Mary Ann read from the letters sent to us by visionary Quakers and nuclear plant operators who sympathized with our attempt to be John Henry to the machine age.

Within that big volume of old and quiet *air*, we sat on the benches through hours of silent worship. We had become present. Even our children were there with us. Unlike a normal conference, we had actually encouraged families to make the journey together.

Then, on the final day, we grappled with a collective statement of nonresistance: a statement of means instead of ends, one that would tell the world we had learned how to turn back the catastrophe of modernity without fighting it. But, despite all the wisdom we gained individually and as a congress, it wasn't to be so simple. There were tense moments as those who believed the old activism could fight globalism and the technosphere had their chance to speak. This momentarily threw our hard-won camaraderie and good feelings into turmoil. But for those of us who had come under God's purpose, it was also a reminder that we were truly embarking on a revolution of *hearts*. Nothing about the situation of modern life will change until we ourselves change. And we cannot change of our own power sufficiently to change the world. The only way is through sacrifice of the self-will. The only pathway out of anger and revenge is love and kindness. And the only way beyond the turmoil of that morning session was to reconnect with God, by waiting in silence.

Suddenly it did become silent, and the bowed heads all around showed that many had learned in these few days a new way—to wait upon the Lord. I was on the raised platform of facing benches, my head down, breathing slowed, when it came to me that if we were to fight fire with fire, we would have to immolate ourselves first of all. A few moments earlier a delegate had passionately argued that it was only right to sabotage the equipment of the loggers of old-growth forests in the Pacific Northwest. But, I thought, how could we destroy someone else's property without first sabotaging all of our cars parked here outside the meetinghouse? Were we any less involved in the physical—let alone cultural or spiritual—destruction of God's handiwork?

Instead of arguing this point, however, I asked God to teach me sacrifice, as required, to change our materialistic and careless society.

A calm had come over the meetinghouse. Slowly people began to stand, one after another, and give eloquent voice to the spirit of nonviolence, loving response, self-denial, and sacrifice. I do not know that every soul was satisfied, but in the end we held hands, all of us, and sang until the rafters shook:

Tis the gift to be simple
'tis the gift to be free
'tis the gift to come down
where we ought to be

all the way through; and then we sang it again:

> And when we find ourselves
> in the place just right
> 'twill be in the valley
> of Love and delight.

and we sang it through still once more:

> When true simplicity is gained
> to bow and to bend we shall not be ashamed
> to turn, turn, will be our delight
> 'til by turning and turning we come 'round right.

The doors opened, the children holding their daffodils crowded up onto the porch, and somewhere in the commotion I had a sense come over me that the least I could do would be to refuse to operate the cars that seem to have rolled over our places and our sense of belonging. Staring wordlessly at the legion of cars parked on the grass all around the meetinghouse, my eyesight seemed to dim, and I received a momentary glimpse—a vision—of how it would be if we would only accept the gifts of simplicity, humility, and love freely offered from above.

This beautiful flash illuminated my heart—and brought me here, to the outskirts of the city of Columbus.

Entering the Capital

Blessed are they which are persecuted for
righteousness' sake: for theirs is the kingdom of
heaven.

It's a splendid day, and even at six-thirty in the morning
the air feels fairly warm. There's a clear sunrise coming
over me as I put my walking stick down onto the sidewalk
that leads west to Columbus. After a few steps I remember
something and stop in the middle of the sidewalk. Strug-
gling out of one shoulder strap, I pull my backpack around
to the front so that I can open one of the pouches and retrieve my driver's license. I want to have it at hand today.
I slip it into my inner coat pocket and take out the Sermon on the Mount to begin memorizing this morning's
beatitude.

So here I am, about to give my license back to the state.

Right now I am going to sit and rest on an ironwork
bench outside the city administration building in Reynoldsburg. This is the first truly prosperous locale I've
been in since leaving home. There's a boom on in America

and in Ohio as I write this, but it hasn't ever made it into the mountainous southeastern part of our state.

Men walking by in coats and ties sort of scowl at me. I'm a bum who somehow wandered out of the downtown Columbus area, they're probably thinking. Well, I do look odd. I'm self-conscious about the walking stick again. Getting up from the bench, I notice that no matter how I grip the crooked staff, it seems to twist in my hand. Maybe it realizes I'm ashamed of it. Turning it upside-down, I see that it has worn its point on one side—perhaps because of the sidewalk it is now pounding against, as opposed to all the time it has spent in the mud and loose gravel along the journey. Sitting back down, I try to even it back up with my pocket knife. The skunky smell of buckeye comes up from the stick, and for a moment I am back in the tree where I freed this limb on New Year's Day. That memory revives my affection for my walking companion, and my courage, too—even though a woman in a suit has just whirled around after passing me to stare first at me, dangerous degenerate, then at the knife. As she hurriedly walks to her car I get back off the bench and begin to sail down the sidewalk, my staff passing from hand to hand like a single oar paddling me into the big city ahead. In fact, I can see it now, a wavering, watery haze of steel straight ahead at the end of the road.

I almost feel that if I turned around and looked back, I would see our little homestead in the same far-off haze; Mary Ann, Tasha, Jack, and Susanna wordlessly wishing me Godspeed. I suppose I could even let crazy Ned wander into the picture in my fancy. Hold thy tongue, old friend.

Picking up my pace again, I think about how I must have looked to those city workers while I sat on the park bench. Did they imagine I was a wild anarchist? It's true that I have an action to perform before the magistrates up ahead, but I'm not doing it as an anarchist. On the contrary, I feel as if I've come under a deeper and more pervasive regulation than I have ever before experienced. I've been filled with God's rule, and I have accepted this fully and freely in a way no anarchic spirit would.

I have also discovered that some of the world's regulations can't be followed—not if I am to stay totally obedient to God. But all in all, I'm no longer hostile to the concept of being under authority. Insofar as they are a reflection of God's will, my church community's standards allow me to willingly yield my daily living to a higher authority than self. In most humdrum instances of law enforcement, I want to be held accountable to the social compacts that restrict uncivil behavior. But my following of a higher law undoubtedly puts me at odds with some human laws, and with the culture of materialism that uses manipulation instead of force.

I simply have to hold the powers of business and government at arm's length. It is for the best, this parting of the ways that I am trying to engineer. I hope it can continue without any hard feelings on either side.

This effort to erase myself from the data banks may appear extreme. But it isn't anarchy or the action of a right-wing militiaman. I'm a member of the antimilitia—a conspiracy of love, not a force for hatred and violence.

I'm just coming here to end my participation in the

games we play in return for our modern privileges. But I'm still confronted with many other restraints on my freedom: as a member of a religious body with a lengthy written Discipline, in my role as husband and father, and in my work as writer, editor, and printer of a magazine. Being a rural homesteader, I often have to dance to the weather's tune. I have to obey the laws that reflect right and wrong behavior.

Why do I accept some kinds of limits and reject others? The difference is that my cherished unofficial life has as its aim to put me into freely chosen obligations that are *reciprocal*.

My church membership, my locally based work life, and my labor in the economy of my household are meeting my physical, mental, and spiritual needs, are in fact weaving these things back together into a whole. As a bonus, these reciprocating obligations continually shield me from the toxic exposure to some of the cultural mediators I previously relied on to meet my needs.

The prison doors were always open. Now I see that anyone can walk right out of the official culture and right into the unofficial one.

By the grace of God.

The road takes me by the turnoff that leads to the state offices of the Bureau of Motor Vehicles. But I want to press on for the last few miles to the center of the capital, to the seat of the government that controls and commands the BMV. I hope to reach the statehouse by noon. Then I'll double back to here. I'll have to hurry, too. A week ago, right before I left, I made an appointment to speak with someone at the BMV about the new high-tech driver's licenses that have been adopted. The person I talked to on the phone said that not one person had complained about the new licenses yet.

I don't intend to complain, either. But maybe my questions (I visit the BMV official today as the editor of *Plain* magazine) will invite some reflection and shed some light on what might be wrong.

Somewhere and sometime in this dehumanizing process, wherein our privacy is invaded not just to expose our human selves but to obliterate it into a meaningless shower of mere data, the doors of the prison will—necessarily—swing shut. Not because of a conspiracy of people or of evil institutions, as in the paranoid's fantasy, but rather as the result of a conspiracy of forms, of structures both physical and digital, that are pushing us into a repressive, bureaucratic corner.

It is time for me to depart from Route 40 for the last time. I'll walk north about two miles and hook up with the main drag through downtown, Broad Street.

Judging by his memoirs, Charles Dickens probably took this same road when he stopped in Columbus on his tour of America in 1842. After an uneventful stagecoach ride from Cincinnati (that in itself was worth remarking on for Dickens, as most of the roads he traveled in Ohio were terrible), Dickens arrived in Columbus on April 20 and relaxed for a while at the Neill House hotel (it's still there). He didn't have much to say about Columbus except that "the town is clean and pretty, and of course is 'going to be' much larger." Those statements are still largely true, and still somewhat all a stranger such as myself can say about Columbus: a nice town with an incredible amount of suburban sprawl surrounding it.

After a few miles of inner-ring suburb trekking, I have come to the urban decay zone, which actually isn't nearly as messed up as some of the rural communities I've passed through to get here. The downtown is coming closer and closer, which makes me happy. I even feel like singing; I'll just sing what I sang on the first day:

> You shall go out with joy
> And be led forth in peace!
> The mountains and the hills
> Shall break forth before you!
> There'll be shouts of joy
> And all the trees of the fields
> Will clap, will clap their hands!

No one can hear me over the sounds of the cars that still zip by in a steady stream, though it's past rush hour. The city teems with pedestrians, the first large influx of fellow walkers I have seen on my trip. Up ahead, past some churches and a large office tower, I can see the capitol dome. I can barely stand here at the Don't Walk sign; only another block to go.

The sign changes and I start out into the crosswalk. In the middle of the crowd crossing from the other side I notice an older man with brown skin and a neatly groomed short white beard staring at me. He walks right toward me, and as we pass, he says in a low, low voice full of warmth, "Welcome, brother. God bless you." In the time it takes me to look behind, he has vanished in the crowd.

Turning left, I run up the steps of the statehouse, through the tall outer doors behind the pillared porticos, and across the marble floor until I am standing under the dome. Then I thank the Lord for leading me here safely.

If you look straight up while kneeling, you can see the stained-glass oculus at the apex of the rotunda's upward sweep. It's the Great Seal of Ohio—mountains, wheat shocks, sunrise, the whole works. A guard who has been watching me pray detaches himself from the curved rotunda wall and starts moving in my direction, so I get up. Over his head the Northwest Ordinance, which preceded statehood, is reproduced on the marble. Article I reads: "No person demeaning himself in a peaceable and orderly manner shall ever be molested on account of his mode of worship or religious sentiments in the said territory."

Now there's nothing to do but drop off my license. The BMV office is actually a few miles back in the direction I came, and I need to get there more quickly than I can walk, because of my appointment to talk to an official for a *Plain* magazine essay. One of the doorways out of the rotunda leads to an underground tunnel that emerges at the cab stand, so I head off in that direction.

I pass through a tiny gift shop in the depths below the statehouse, all watery glass and natural wood, with Ohio-related trinkets displayed on the aqua-hued glass shelves. It will just take a minute to find some keepsakes for Tasha,

Jack, and Susanna: cowhide bookmarks stamped with the buckeye leaf. And here a small collection of beautiful stones, one from each of the five geologic regions of the state. There's our eastern Ohio flint, which the Indians once treasured. For a moment I hold all of them up to the aqua-colored light, wondering at their polished smoothness. Then I take my staff in my hand, pour the five stones into their leather carrying pouch, and get into the checkout line.

Rushing onward, I have to climb some stairs to reach the portal opening onto the street. I barely raise my hand before a taxi breaks out of traffic and slides to the curb in front of me. As I am getting in, the cab driver turns around, smiles, and says, "I recognized you as a friend by your staff."

What does he mean by that? It turns out he's from Nigeria, where many of the men carry a walking stick. So we have something in common. As soon as I have given him the address of the Bureau of Motor Vehicles and settled into my seat, the driver—Samuel, as he has introduced himself—does the typical midwestern cabbie thing and launches right into a story. I sit back and imagine the scene as he describes it.

"I always pick up you Amish people," he begins, his smile framed in the rearview mirror.

"Soon after I came here from Nigeria and became a taxi driver, I was waiting one time outside the bus station when this group of very big men came out, surrounded my cab, and then got in. I didn't have time to decide anything— they were just in, front and back, and right away they made me really nervous, not only because they were so big, compared to people the size of me and you, but because they looked so rough and tough. Grim, and dressed in black with big black hats. There was an older one with a gray beard, and he told me where they were going—it was out of the city, about fifty miles away. Hey, that's a good fare. So I started driving, even though I was really scared that they might be bank robbers or American Mafia bosses.

"The whole drive they never talked, except muttering sometimes in another language to each other. By now it was nighttime. The old man had me turn off the main road onto a gravel lane, and it was pitch black out there. No streetlights, no telephone poles, just houses with no lights and big, dark buildings that looked like warehouses. Man, was I scared! Jesse, the old guy, told me to stop in front of a house, and all the younger ones—he called them his "boys"—piled out of the cab and went in, while he told me the fare money was in the house and he'd be right back.

"Well, I waited a long time there in the dark, all the time I'm thinking, What am I doing, sitting here waiting to be robbed or killed? So I turned around in the road and stepped on it. Man, I flew back to Columbus. At the bus station I saw a Nigerian friend of mine who's a driver, and I told him all about my escape from these evil guys.

"Oh, he laughed at me. He laughed and laughed. He said, 'Samuel, those were Amish! They're farmers, they're good Christians, like you and me. They don't hurt anybody. They live the simple way, and don't even have electricity on their farms. I drive them home from the bus station all the time.' "

Samuel looks at me in the mirror again, shaking his head with a sheepish grin.

"Now I always pick up you Amish. I got to earn back that fare I turned down. . . . Your stop's coming up."

I have to cash a traveler's check today, so I ask him to let me off at the bank that sits in front of the BMV's parking lot. I'm still laughing along with Samuel as I get out, but I have to correct him and say that I'm actually not Amish, I'm a Quaker, and not a lifelong one at that.

"You chose it?" he asks more soberly. "Well, to live that way, to choose it after living the other way, ahh," he says, waving his hand over my head and brushing away such distinctions as Amish versus Quaker, "that makes you even more so." A smile again, and he pulls away from the curb.

Inside the bank I am immediately confronted by photocopied warnings taped above the tellers' cages: DRIVER'S LICENSE ID NO LONGER ACCEPTED FOR CHECK CASHING.

Sailing right through and out the other door, I make my way to the BMV building, passing by an entry guard and two security cameras before reaching a desk manned by three state patrolmen. I confirm my appointment.

Don—my interview subject—ushers me into his office, and I begin asking questions and taking notes (although I'm really here to witness to *him,* the only way to do so is to let him explain himself).

He begins by describing the driver's license as the most common form of identification people carry. It's also the one most often used to conduct fraud. That's been the chief problem with the old, "analog" license I have in my pocket, he says. It was much too easy to fake it and use it to commit crimes.

"The banks have put a lot of pressure on the motor vehicles officials to make the license more secure," he claims. The digital features of the new card were propelled by the banks in particular. Now, according to Don, almost everyone has a much more fraud-resistant, computer-linked identity document.

As he is saying this, he keeps gesturing out the large window behind his desk to where the bank sits beyond the parking lot. I mention as mildly as possible that this particular bank appears unconvinced about the safety of the new license IDs.

"No, really? I was in there last week and there weren't any signs up!" he says, shooting an accusing glance in the bank's direction.

It is true, he acknowledges with a sigh, that fraud will always be with us. "As soon as we bring out a new technology—in the 1950s or the 1990s—people will take advantage of it."

Don relaxes into his chair and begins to explain how the whole digital license scheme came about. The technology was originally developed by the federal government to block interstate truck drivers from carrying multiple operator's licenses.

"We built a commercial driver's information system, shared by all the states," he said. "The files are computerized, so the license had to be computer-readable."

Ohio and thirty-five other states then applied to citizen-drivers this apparatus designed to control the heavily regulated trucking industry. The participating states share technical standards that allow them to access one another's data. The file of an Ohioan detained by California police can be had by swiping the license through a reader. Banks, video stores, and a lot of retail outlets already use the license and computers to establish identity and transact business. Some states have begun to incorporate micro-chips into their licenses to store even more data.

I mention to Don that it sounds as if, in the service of combating crime and providing order and convenience, a de facto national identity card has simply appeared. I get a nod and a wary look.

I say that this appears to have happened absent any na-tional legislation or amendment of the Bill of Rights. For our own good, we'll be protected from having our identity stolen. But the act of protecting it has made it public. And a purely accessible, public identity is no identity at all.

"It sounds like," I say to Don, "your effort to save our control over our individual identities has opened the way for them to be destroyed."

I have assumed that Don figured me for a nut even be-fore I got here, and I have been trying to work against that by being as quiet and genuinely friendly as I can. My calmness and measured tone seem to have had a positive effect; Don isn't disagreeing with my analysis. I go on to explain to him my personal objection to more efficient methods of data gathering: Using technology to wed my official self more closely to my real self is like tagging my ear with a number. It makes me feel like a domesticated steer, and it changes who I am. In fact, by treating me as data—something I am not—it confuses and makes me *less sure* of who I am. Don's eyes are brighter. He's looking at me intently, but it isn't possible to guess what he might be thinking.

"Don, how has American life changed over your lifetime?"

"People are much, much more mobile," he says, shaking his head. "And less conscious of their freedom to go anywhere they please."

Still shaking his head, he continues, "College students expect to head for Florida on spring break—and their parents think nothing of taking long-distance trips on a moment's notice." Yes, he has seen in his fifty-eight years a disintegration of family, and of the home as the center of family life. Young and old seem to be whirling apart into separate worlds.

And so we sit quietly, pondering that thought, our conversation ending on this sad note. Now my mission with Don is almost accomplished. As we stand to say goodbye, I tell Don that I've come here not only to question him about the new driver's license, but also to give up my own older model instead of getting a new one.

I have come to tell him this because he is, after all, the systems administrator for the small laminated cardboard rectangle I have carried in my pocket for over twenty years. If anyone needs to know that my conscience will no longer allow me to keep it, surely it is he.

As soon as I tell him that I plan to cancel my driving privileges at the county license bureau downstairs, I feel stupid—like I did at prayer meeting back in Barnesville. Don is giving me a strange look as we shake hands, almost as if he is afraid of me. I don't think he regards me as dangerous or crazy now, so it's not that kind of look. I've sensed his own misgivings about the license and even about our society, and I have to wonder if he isn't afraid of himself, of what my action tells him about his own failure to resist.

Or maybe it isn't fear at all, but rather that he is bestowing a solemn and fearful blessing as I prepare to void my contract with his employer.

I feel surer and surer still of my calling as I slip down the stairs. Making my way once again through the corridors of security apparatus and around to the entrance of the county license bureau, I feel a certain comforting familiarity in what I'm doing. The truth is that I have done all of this many times before, cancelling or avoiding participation in the official life of our society. The results, privacy-wise, have always been positive.

For example, Mary Ann and I were married before God and thirty-five witnesses, but it felt out of place to invite the government to our wedding. We never got around to filing a civil certificate of marriage, as required by law.

Our first child was born without benefit of hospital bureaucracy. She came into the world unofficially, privately, at our home, attended by a lay midwife (also illegal in our state).

Unfortunately, I made the mistake of filling out a birth certificate I had obtained through unauthorized channels; I was under the impression that I could present this to the county registrar just as a formality. However, a few days later Mildred—the health department nurse—showed up on our porch with a mandate to examine our newborn. She wanted to insert an immunization needle, stab our baby's heel to take blood, put something in her eyes "to prevent syphilis."

Then she asked, "And by the way, who did you say your midwife was?"

In the end, she got nothing that she came for, but we'd had to sign a form claiming religious objection before she would leave.

Birth records are public, so the carefully (how could I be so dumb!) completed birth certificate soon yielded a large crop of direct-mail advertisements for disposable diapers, baby formula, and subscription forms for what I can only describe as antiparenting magazines. Later on came personalized birthday cards promoting disposable training pants and "educational" videos for our toddler.

Least expected, however, was the fact that filing the birth certificate meant that our baby was automatically issued a federal identification number for Social Security. It seemed to Mary Ann and me that babies ought not to have to take part in a government program—but ours had already been enrolled. The card arrived in time for her one-month birthday.

In a practical sense, none of these instantaneous hook-ups to the corporate and bureaucratic worlds had any real effect on our child. No person outside of our family and community really had any personal knowledge of or interest in her. But our daughter and her Social Security number have created an official existence, subject to being tracked and "helped" by government and business. There may be nothing sinister about that, but the results are anything but benign.

And there is a more aggressive side to numbering babies. The boy ones grow up and are brought into military service by that number. In case you didn't already know, we're a family of pacifists, utterly opposed to war.

What to do? In this case, we just had to break the law. I never filed any more birth certificates. The rest of our children after the first are unknown to the government. We cannot claim these undocumented children on our tax return form—they don't "exist"—so we are paying a hefty annual penalty for our disobedience.

One reason I am here today at the BMV office is that I am coming to an ever deeper level of disobedience to our laws, to the point where I am ready to slip free of the essential covenants. We are close to putting ourselves out of the moneymaking, taxpaying cycle completely, which ought to drop us off the radar screen. We'll all be better for it when it happens.

I wonder what good thing will come out of my letting go of the state's driving privilege. I have a feeling that it will enhance the need I have for others—a negative possibility in the larger culture, but a truly positive one in the culture I have claimed as my own.

Take, for example, the question of the birth certificate. Every child needs to be welcomed into the world by a circle of people who will nurture and protect that new life. I had mistakenly thought that filing a birth certificate would fill part of the ceremonial function of welcoming Tasha. At that time, Mary Ann and I still lived without a close religious community, or even a neighborhood. As we realized what it is that children need, wanting our children to be truly welcomed and enfolded by others was one of the things that prompted us to seek Christian community.

And each of our children's births has been upheld by our community, both ceremonially, as their arrivals have been briefly noted in the minutes of our Friends business meetings, and concretely, as they have been loved and cared for by family, friends, and brethren. Their identities and their souls have been made secure in the reciprocity of our relationships with others.

Now it's time to secure my own ability to know where I am and where I'm going. After I give back my license, I'll have one more night away from home. Tomorrow I'll take the bus back, a two-hour trip from Columbus to Barnesville—time enough to memorize the last beatitude. Then I'll drop my staff and pack and begin picking up my precious ones, hoisting them into the air one by one.

But first I have to step through this license bureau door.

Back Home

Blessed are ye, when men shall revile you, and persecute you, and shall say all manner of evil against you falsely, for my sake. Rejoice, and be exceeding glad: for great is your reward in heaven: for so persecuted they the prophets which were before you.

It is the first day of the week, and I'm sitting on a meeting-house bench along with the others in Bible study today. The text this week happens to be from the fifth chapter of the Book of Matthew: "Blessed are the pure of heart, for they shall see God." And "Ye are the light of the world. A city set on a hill cannot be hid. . . . Neither do men light a candle, and put it under a bushel, but on a candlestick: and it giveth light to all that are in the house."

After the session ends with a prayer, someone asks about my trip. I wonder aloud if they would like to hear what happened when I completed the task for which I had gone on my pilgrimage, and the answer is yes.

———

The county license office in Columbus turned out to be a large, low-ceilinged affair, partitioned by a counter into the seating area and the space taken up by the clerks and their bureaucratic paraphernalia of desks, machines, filing cabinets, and several surveillance cameras. A video loop about the state highway patrol played on the monitor sitting on the counter, as the clerks occasionally bellowed a number or a name.

I pulled a ticket—B-1—from the machine and took a seat in a row of chairs. An eight- or nine-year-old child in the row in front of me hopped on and off her older sister's knee. As the seats continued filling, a pleasant-looking young woman sat beside my hat, which I'd placed on the chair next to me. B-14—she had a long wait ahead.

"Excuse me," the older girl in front of us said to an angry-faced young man sitting down in her little sister's chair. "That seat is taken."

His answering volley of profanity and threats transformed the room, alerting all of us in the seating area to his utter rage and hostility. But eventually he did move over a few seats, muttering death and mayhem. Before the crisis had passed, I had enough time to ready myself to help the girls escape him, but it wasn't necessary after all. Looking up at the surveillance cameras, I remember thinking how terrifically responsible we are for one another, whether we know it or not. Even though the waiting-room cameras of modern life confuse us with their promise of protection, we are yet responsible for one another. Back home, 120 miles away, some of us were working on accepting that need to care for one another.

Into the stunned silence a voice sweetly queried: "Where are you from?"

"Heaven," I shakily replied, turning to my waiting room companion. "Well, Barnesville," I corrected myself.

"My grandmother lives in Barnesville, and I've seen people there dressed like you. I've wondered if I would be welcome to attend a Quaker meeting."

Yes, of course she would be welcome to attend, I assured her. And then the clerk shouted, "Be One!"

After I canceled my license and signed the form, I waited outside the building for a taxi. Suddenly I remembered something. Brushing past the cameras and the patrolman at the door, I ran back down the hall to the license office.

"Meeting for worship is at ten-thirty," I told my new friend.

That's the end of the story. On the bench across from mine in Bible study, Carol laughs and says, "Maybe that's really why you had to walk to Columbus, Scott. To tell that woman she was welcome to visit us."

Maybe it was. In Columbus I gave up the privilege of having a digital identity. Living this other life, a plain life, is allowing me to strive to be what the Lord wants: purely myself, the same on the inside as on the outside. In that grounded, authentic place of being, I know that I can hear Him calling us, and I can pass that calling on.

Bible study is over, and meeting for worship is about to begin. People are standing and stretching; some are already centering in the waiting silence, fixing their minds and hearts on Jesus Christ, our Lord and Master. The outer door opens and my children come running into the room, followed more slowly by my wife and a new visitor to our meeting.

Acknowledgments

Thank heaven for Ginny Faber, who snuck me in past the guardians of the Bottom Line whilst circumventing the marketplace Cult of the Invisible Hand in order to bring *A Plain Life* before the public.

I am equally thankful for Jason Zuzga's advocacy on behalf of my book, as well as his close readings, helpful suggestions, and constant encouragement. That he happens to be the only person in Manhattan publishing to have cared for and driven horses in harness only goes to show how blessed has been this little enterprise.

Victoria Shoemaker placed the book with Ginny Faber, and Greg Tobin at Ballantine kept it on the publishing schedule. I appreciate their efforts. I am grateful to the Foundation for Deep Ecology for supporting the early stages of the writing of this book, and to the Friends Center at Olney for lending a peaceful place to remember and tell the story.

Westminster-John Knox Press graciously allowed the quotes from *The Gospel of Matthew, Volume 1* by William Barclay, and Houghton Mifflin permitted me to excerpt passages from George Stewart's *U.S. 40*. I also thank the editors who published some of this prose as essays, and my friend Chuck Trapkus for his artwork.

Of course I could not have written *A Plain Life* without the help and patience of my family. I am especially beholden to Mary Ann, Natasha, and Jack for filling in at chore time while I was walking and when I later needed time alone to write.

My expression of gratitude would not be complete without acknowledging two stories that prepared me for my walk to Columbus. Lee Hoinacki's *El Camino: The Way* inspired me with the historical roots of Christian pilgrimage. The Bible story of David, a boy with nothing in his arsenal but a shepherd's bag of stones, has taught me to lean on the Lord of All in every contest with giants.

About the Author

SCOTT SAVAGE is the editor of *Plain* magazine and a cofounder of the Center for Plain Living. He is also the editor of *A Plain Reader: Essays on Making a Simple Life*. He organized the Second Luddite Congress in Barnesville, Ohio, where he now resides.